Jill Dawson was born in 1962 in Durham and grew up in Yorkshire. She is a poet, editor and short-story writer, the editor of *School Tales*, and author of *How Do I Look?* She has been a contributor to various books and anthologies including *In the Gold of Flesh* (poetry) and *Erotica: Writing by Women* (short fiction). In 1992 she won an Eric Gregory Award for her poetry. She has been writer-in-residence at Doncaster, and more recently, writer-in-residence at Fareham College, Hampshire. She lives in Hackney with her partner and their young son.

THE VIRAGO BOOK OF
WICKED VERSE

Edited by
Jill Dawson

Published by VIRAGO PRESS Limited 1992
20–23 Mandela Street, London NW1 0HQ

Reprinted 1992, 1993 (twice)

Acknowledgements for all copyright material are given
on pages 161–8, which constitute an extension of
this copyright page

A CIP catalogue record for this title
is available from the British Library

Printed in Great Britain

For my sister, Debra, with love

Acknowledgements

I am indebted to Andrew Graham, himself a poet, for his considerable contribution to this book in terms of poems found and suggested, hours of research, and expertise on poets from a huge diversity of cultures. I'd like to thank Melanie Silgardo at Virago for calmly steering me through the administrative tasks of this anthology and for her warm and professional approach to editing, and all the poets, translators and publishers who granted me permission to reproduce the poems in this collection.

My thanks are also due to the staff at the Poetry Library, most notably Louise Granger, Tim Brown, Simon Smith and Dolores Conway for their patience with my endless enquiries; to Kate, Karen, Stella, Gladys Mary Coles and Linda Rhiumens for pointing me towards poems and poets; to Stewart and all those at Stepping Stones Childcare co-operative for practical and emotional support; and to Lewis, for inspiration.

Contents

'The bush catches fire'

'Queens of the underworld'

'If they can't take a joke . . .'

Introduction

When I set out to gather poems by women which could be described as 'wicked', I was aware that I was on a path taking me away from the places where poetry by women has been traditionally allowed to travel; away from much love poetry, romantic poetry, poetry in praise of nature, children, and 'the hearth', poetry by women waiting patiently for soldiers to return, expressing no criticism of the war or system that sent their sons and lovers away; poetry which in form or subject matter did not shake the concept of woman as custodian of virtue – good in herself and good in what she chooses to write and how she chooses to write it.

The Oxford Concise defines wicked as, amongst other things, 'playfully mischievous' or 'roguish'. Much of the poetry originally submitted for the anthology was not 'roguish' in the least, but instead fell prey to the same, tired old judgements. Its subject was women behaving 'wickedly' in the conventional sense. This usually amounted to acting on their appetites, whether sleeping with another woman's husband, or eating a lot of chocolate eclairs. The tone was reminiscent of the cream cakes advertising slogan of a few years ago: 'naughty but nice', which was very much aimed at a guilt-ridden woman consumer. Any poems about eating chocolate were promptly returned.

That women have been the custodians of morality in life and are expected to be so in art is even more apparent when we speak of mothers: 'Mothers have as powerful an influence over the welfare of future generations, as all other earthly causes combined . . . When our land is filled with *pious* and *patriotic* mothers, then will it be filled with virtuous and patriotic men. The world's redeeming influence, under the blessing of the Holy Spirit, must come from a mother's lips' (*emphasis mine*). (The American Tract Society of the 1830s).

I spent months ferreting out verse which was more subversive. What began to surface was an abundance of poetry by women in gloriously rebellious, angry and wicked mood. Stevie Smith's poem 'Lightly Bound' is a startling rejection of the honey-dipped picture of motherhood, and Liz Lochhead in 'Everybody's Mother' dissects the persistent myth of the mother with a ruthless poet's scalpel.

In a collection which spans Sappho to the present day, context is of course relevant in determining if a poem is wicked. Whilst it is easy to imagine that the average 17th century reader *would* have been scandalised by the poet Aphra Behn declaring her willingness to sexual delights, it is both surprising and telling that in England in the 1990s, Fiona Pitt-Kethley continues to shock the literary establishment with her bawdy sense of humour and plain speaking about sex. (For a time Pitt-Kethley had great difficulty finding a publisher for her work. One poetry collection was refused on the grounds that it contained 'too many perversions'.) A modern poem like 'Seduction' by Nikki Giovanni echoes Behn's as a song of desire, but this time the poet has to get beyond the political ideology of her prospective lover, not the prevailing moral climate.

Maria Jastrzębska's poem 'Which of us Wears the Trousers' is a witty jibe at hypocrisy and prejudice, just as the Chinese folk poem (possibly from as long ago as 1200 BC) which begins 'I'm eighteen, he's nine' is a furious attack on the system of the match-makers and the sexual rules of the time. It might be argued that the poems celebrating sex written by the Japanese women of court Ono no Komachi and Izumi Shikibu, cannot be described as wicked at all, because love affairs were the permitted, even expected subjects for the women of the ancient Heian court to write about. However, the poems have been included because they have a simplicity and naturalness which speaks candidly of women's sexual feelings and which contemporary poems about sex sometimes lack.

There are more than a few jibes at the male anatomy contained within this compilation. Vicki Raymond's poem 'On Seeing the First Flasher' asks 'when shalt thou find a partner to thy game,/ a maid whose pleasure is to stand and watch?' and for an answer Sylvia Plath's virgin protagonist in *The Bell Jar* springs immediately to mind, as she remarks: 'The only thing I could think of was turkey neck and turkey gizzard and I felt very depressed.'

The American poet Adrienne Rich reminded us in the seventies in her essay, 'When We Dead Awaken: Writing as Re-Vision' that of course, women who write poetry have been, and remain, mainly a middle-class bunch: 'Like Virginia Woolf, I am aware of the women who are not with us here because they are washing the dishes and looking after the children . . . not to mention women who went on the streets last night in order to feed their children.' One way to widen the scope of an anthology such as this is to include as I have, folk poems, rhymes ('Diamond Lily' is a good example), ballads and songs.

Gathering the material for this book has been pure joy. I wish I could say the same of the administrative task of agreeing payment and permissions with all the poets to be included. The inevitable financial constraints of producing an anthology have naturally resulted in some omissions; poets who have been offered in tiny bite-sized pieces and others not at all. It was similarly impossible to be representative of every culture or nationality, but I did, in collating this material read as widely as possible, following up all sorts of unlikely leads and suggestions, to my lasting advantage; since it introduced me to poets and poems hitherto unknown.

Lastly, definitions and explanations of the term 'wicked' were immaterial to a group of people I was working with at the time of compiling this anthology. The children of a North London School – Queen's Park Community School – where I taught creative writing, understood the word to describe something quite different. 'Wicked' to them is a term meaning funny, good, deft, sexy, *awesome* . . . and it is in this spirit, more than any other, that the anthology is intended.

Jill Dawson
1992

'The clitoris in my throat'

Sappho

'IF YOU ARE SQUEAMISH'

If you are squeamish

Don't prod the
beach rubble

Translated by Mary Barnard

Ntozake Shange

From WOW . . . YR JUST LIKE A MAN!

he said hangin out with her waz just like hangin out witta man/she
cd drink & talk pungently/ even tell a risqué joke or two/ more n
that/ she cd talk abt art/ & that musta made her a man/ cuz she sure
cdnt scratch her balls/or pee further n him/or fuck a tiny fella in
the ass/ she didn't have a football letter/ & she cdnt talk abt how
many women she'd had/but then we dont know that either/all we
know is he said she waz just like a fella/& here she waz thinkin she
waz as good as any woman/which to her meant she waz as good as
any fella/but that's an idea without a large following in these parts/
any way the way the relationship evolved/ he & this woman he waz
thinkin waz like a fella/well they worked together alla the time/
had poetry readings/ did exercises/ saw shows/ cut-up everybody
else's work on the phone/ & you must know since/ she hadta be a
fella to understand/ probably you awready guessed/ their shared
craft waz poetry/ cuz words/ are a man's thing/ you know/ the
craftsmen/ the artisan/ the artist/ they are all in men/ why else wd
you haveta put 'ess' on the end of every damn thing/ if it waznt to
signify when/a woman waz doin something that men do/

Sylvia Kantaris

From THE POET'S WIFE

I help him by taking on the boring jobs
like sorting, filing, typing out and sending to mags.
Try the Big Ones˜first, he says, but all their editors
are handicapped. (The slips say they're 'unable to publish'.)

The others sometimes shift a paper-clip a bit
before they send them back with a form for a sub.
You have to pay to be a poet, but he packed in his job
after laying six quid out to win five, in a comp.

I don't trouble him with trivialities like FIS
because he has to keep his mind clear and sometimes,
my God, a single line will take up to a week
but if it doesn't seem a moment's thought it's wasted ink.

I like those lines and can't think why he doesn't
write them down and make the best poem ever yet.
Possibly because he uses ballpoint?
It's hard for him when rhymes won't come out right.

Poetry's like ironing, he said – you have to smooth
the creases out. I just get on with it.
Usually he ends up with a crumpled sheet in spite
of getting all steamed up. I'm glad I'm not a poet.

You have to work like mad to make the sentences
sound senseless at the moment, so he writes
'surprising' lines that I can't fathom such as
'Ears like elephantine hand-grenades'.

I don't see the point of it, but he says poets
gaze into a crystal ball like seers and the mists
eventually clear up so that, instead of seeing ordinary leaves,
they see words decomposing in the woods.

Eunice de Souza

POEM FOR A POET

It pays to be a poet.
You don't have to pay prostitutes.

Marie has spiritual thingummies.
Write her a poem about the
Holy Ghost. Say:
'Marie, my frequent sexual encounters
represent more than an attempt
to find mere physical fulfilment.
They are a poet's struggle to
transcend the self
and enter into
communion
with the world.'

Marie's eyes will glow.
Pentecostal flames will descend.
The Holy Ghost will tremble inside her.
She will babble in strange tongues:

'O Universal Lover
in a state of perpetual erection!
Let me too enter into
communion with the world
through thee.'

Ritu loves music and
has made a hobby of psychology.
Undergraduate, and better still,
uninitiated.
Write her a poem about woman flesh.
Watch her become oh so womanly and grateful.
Giggle with her about
horrid mother keeping an eye
on the pair, the would-be babes
in the wood, and everything will be
so idyllic, so romantic
so *intime*

Except, that you, big deal,
are forty-six
and know what works
with whom.

Rachel Annand Taylor

ART AND WOMEN

The triumph of Art compels few womenkind;
    And these are yoked like slaves to Eros' car –
No victors they! Yet ours the Dream behind,
    Who are nearer to the gods than poets are.
For with the silver moons we wax and wane,
    And with the roses love most woundingly,
And, wrought from flower to fruit with dim rich pain,
    The Orchard of the Pomegranates are we.
For with Demeter still we seek the Spring,
    With Dionysus tread the sacred Vine,
Our broken bodies still imagining
    The mournful Mystery of the Bread and Wine –
And Art, that fierce confessor of the flowers,
Desires the secret spice of those veiled hours.

Anne French

THE DANGERS OF ART

So I ended up in your book? Thanks.
Marvellous to see myself undressed
and systematically examined in the clear

unblinking light of your malice.
What a judge of character you are.
How helpful I find it to see my excesses

laid out like used knickers. The rows
you've subjected to mature analysis. Pique
– as you describe it – makes me bicker

but you remain unmoved, splendid
and gracious in the face of it. The reader
will applaud your great forbearance.

That night I importuned you . . . how right
you were to turn me down. Think what ill
would have come of it if you'd complied.

With such an eye for detail as yours, who
could be ungrateful? My intellect (so-called,
how generous), my drinking, my passions, my bad

language laid out in shades of purple. Only
you would tell the precise degree of sag my
breasts had then – no doubt they're worse

since you last saw them – the colour
of my knitting, my recipe for pesto,
my proclivities. What is a friend,

after all, but someone you can trust
with the niceties? How can I thank you enough?
Regard this poem as payment in kind.

Maya Angelou

IMPECCABLE CONCEPTION

I met a Lady Poet
who took for inspiration
colored birds, and whispered words,
a lover's hesitation.

A falling leaf could stir her.
A wilting, dying rose

would make her write, both day and night,
the most rewarding prose.

She'd find a hidden meaning
in every pair of pants,
then hurry home to be alone
and write about romance.

Mary Barber

CONCLUSION OF A LETTER TO THE REV. MR. C—

'Tis time to conclude; for I make it a rule
To leave off all writing, when *Con.* comes from school.
He dislikes what I've written, and says I had better
To send what he calls a poetical letter.
To this I reply'd, you are out of your wits;
A letter in verse would put him in fits;
He thinks it a crime in a woman to read –
Then what would he say should your counsel succeed?

I pity poor *Barber*, his wife's so romantic:
A letter in rhyme! – Why, the woman is frantic.
This reading the Poets has quite turn'd her head!
On my life, she should have a dark room and straw bed.
I often heard say, that *St Patrick* took care,
No poisonous creature should live in this air:
He only regarded the body, I find;
But *Plato* consider'd who poison'd the mind.
Would they'd follow his precepts, who sit at the helm,
And drive poetasters from out of the realm!

Her husband has surely a terrible life;
There's nothing I dread, like a verse-writing wife:
Defend me, ye powers, from that fatal curse;
Which must heighten the plagues of *for better for worse*!

May I have a wife that will dust her own floor;

And not the fine minx recommended by *More*.
(That he was a dotard, is granted, I hope,
Who dy'd for asserting the rights of the Pope.)
If ever I marry, I'll choose me a spouse,
That shall *serve* and *obey*, as she's bound by her vows;
That shall, when I'm dressing, attend like a valet;
Then go to the kitchen, and study my palate.
She has wisdom enough, that keeps out of the dirt,
And can make a good pudding, and cut out a shirt.
What good's in a dame that will pore on a book?
No! – Give me the wife that shall save me a cook.

Thus far I had written – Then turn'd to my son,
To give him advice, ere my letter was done.
My son, should you marry, look out for a wife,
That's fitted to lighten the labours of life.
Be sure, wed a woman you thoroughly know,
And shun, above all things, a *housewifely shrew*;
That would fly to your study, with fire in her looks,
And ask what you got by your poring on books;
Thinking dressing of dinner the height of all science,
And to peace and good humour bid open defiance.

Avoid the fine lady, whose beauty's her care;
Who sets a high price on her shape, and her air;
Who in dress, and in visits, employs the whole day;
And longs for the ev'ning, to sit down to play.

Choose a woman of wisdom, as well as good breeding,
With a turn, at least no aversion, to reading:
In the care of her person, exact and refin'd;
Yet still, let her principal care be her mind:
Who can, when her family cares give her leisure,
Without the dear cards, pass an ev'ning with pleasure;
In forming her children to virtue and knowledge,
Nor trust, for that care, to a school, or a college:
By learning made humble, not thence taking airs,
To despise, or neglect, her domestic affairs:
Nor think her less fitted for doing her duty,
By knowing its reasons, its use, and its beauty.

When you gain her affection, take care to preserve it,
Lest others persuade her, you do not deserve it.
Still study to heighten the joys of her life;
Nor treat her the worse, for her being your wife.
If in judgement she errs set her right, without pride:
'Tis the province of insolent fools, to deride.
A husband's first praise, is a Friend and Protector:
Then change not these titles, for Tyrant and Hector.
Let your person be neat, unaffectedly clean,
Tho' alone with your wife the whole day you remain.
Choose books, for her study, to fashion her mind,
To emulate those who excell'd of her kind.
Be religion the principal care of your life,
As you hope to be blest in your children and wife;
So you, in your marriage, shall gain its true end;
And find, in your wife, a Companion and Friend.

OluYomi Majekodunmi

EVERYTIME

You've read the book.
You've read the story.
So what did it say?
– Tell me.
Who wrote it?
And why?
Who for?
And why?
What man?
And why?
Why do you use his words?
And why?
Why do you believe?
And why?
Everytime you speak
And why

– do you use him on me?

Everytime you speak

Your trousers are too big
for me to wear.
Here you are.
Take Them!
and your book.
You are the story.

Dorothy Parker

SONG OF PERFECT PROPRIETY

Oh, I should like to ride the seas.
   A roaring buccaneer;
A cutlass banging at my knees,
   A dirk behind my ear.
And when my captives' chains would clank
   I'd howl with glee and drink,
And then fling out the quivering plank
   And watch the beggars sink.

I'd like to straddle gory decks,
   And dig in laden sands,
And know the feel of throbbing necks
   Between my knotted hands.
Oh, I should like to strut and curse
   Among my blackguard crew . . .
But I am writing little verse,
   As little ladies do.

Oh, I should like to dance and laugh
   And pose and preen and sway,
And rip the hearts of men in half,
   And toss the bits away.
I'd like to view the reeling years
   Through unastonished eyes,

And dip my finger-tips in tears,
  And give my smiles for sighs.

I'd stroll beyond the ancient bounds,
  And tap at fastened gates,
And hear the prettiest of sound –
  The clink of shattered fates.
My slaves I'd like to bind with thongs
  That cut and burn and chill . . .
But I am writing little songs,
  As little ladies will.

Nina Cassian

LICENTIOUSNESS

Letters fall from my words
as teeth might fall from my mouth.
Lisping? Stammering? Mumbling?
Or the last silence?
Please God take pity
on the roof of my mouth,
on my tongue,
on my glottis,
on the clitoris in my throat
vibrating, sensitive, pulsating,
exploding in the orgasm of Romanian.

Translated by Brenda Walker and Andrea Deletant

Joan Larkin

'VAGINA' SONNET

Is 'vagina' suitable for use
in a sonnet? I don't suppose so.

A famous poet told me, 'Vagina's ugly.'
Meaning, of course, the *sound* of it. In poems.
Meanwhile he inserts his penis frequently
into his verse, calling it, seriously, 'My
Penis'. It *is* short, I know, and dignified.
I mean of course the sound of it. In poems.
This whole thing is unfortunate, but petty,
like my hangup concerning English Dept memos
headed 'Mr/Mrs/Miss' – only a fishbone
In the throat of the revolution –
a waste of brains – to be concerned about
this minor issue of my cunt's good name.

Gillian Allnutt

ODE

'To depict a (bicycle) you must first come to love (it)' Alexander Blok

I swear by every rule in the bicycle
owner's manual

that I love you, I, who have repeatedly,
painstakingly,

with accompanying declaration of despair,
tried to repair

you, to patch things up,
to maintain a workable relationship.

I have spent sleepless nights
in pondering your parts – those private

and those that all who walk the street
may look at –

wondering what makes you tick
over smoothly, or squeak.

O my trusty steed,
my rusty three-speed,

I would feed you the best oats
if oats

were applicable.
Only linseed oil

will do
to nourish you.

I want
so much to paint

you,
midnight blue

mudgutter black
and standing as you do, ironic

at the rail
provided by the Council –

beautiful
the sun caught in your back wheel –

or at home in the hall, remarkable
among other bicycles,

your handlebars erect.
Allow me to depict

you thus. And though I can't do justice
to your true opinion of the surface

of the road –
put into words

the nice distinctions that you make
among the different sorts of tarmac –

still I'd like to set the record of our travels straight.
I'd have you know that

not with three-in-one
but with my own

heart's
spittle I anoint your moving parts.

Lynn Peters

I SUSPECT

I suspect
There would be more poems
About sex
If it rhymed with more than
Pecks
Necks
Erects and ejects.

This begins to sound promising.
I may write one.

Alison Fell

IN CONFIDENCE
(for the Writers' Group)

– An orgasm is like an anchovy,
she says,
little, long, and very salty.

– No, it's a caterpillar,
undulating, fat and sweet.

– A sunburst, says the third,
an exploding watermelon:
I had one at Christmas.

– Your body betrays, she says,
one way or another.
Rash and wriggling, it comes
and comes, while your mind
says lie low, or go.

– Or else it snarls and shrinks
to the corner of its cage

while your mind, consenting,
whips it on and out,
out in the open
and *so* free.

– As for me,
says the last,
if I have them brazen
with birthday candles,
with water faucets
or the handles of Toby Jugs,
I don't care who knows it.
But how few I have –
keep *that* in the dark.

Wisława Szymborska

IN PRAISE OF DREAMS

In my dreams
I paint like Vermeer van Delft.

I speak fluent Greek
and not only with the living.

I drive a car
which obeys me.

I am talented,
I write long, great poems.

I hear voices
no less than the major saints.

You would be amazed
at my virtuosity on the piano.

I float through the air as is proper,
that is, all by myself.

Falling from the roof
I can softly land on green grass.

I don't find it hard
to breathe under water.

I can't complain:
I've succeeded in discovering Atlantis.

I'm delighted that just before dying
I always manage to wake.

Right after the outbreak of war
I turn over on my favorite side.

I am but I need not
be a child of my time.

A few years ago
I saw two suns.

And the day before yesterday a penguin.
With the utmost clarity.

Translated by Magnus J. Krynski and Robert A. Maguire

Anna Swir

PROLOGUE
Woman Speaks to Her Thigh

It's due entirely to your beauty
that I can take part
in the rites of love.

The mystical ecstasies,
the small betrayals exquisite
as scarlet lipstick,
the perverse rococo
convolutions of the psyche,
the sweetness of sensual longing
choking the breath in my breast,

the craters of despair
descending to the world's utmost depths –
all these I owe to you.

I ought to whip you tenderly each day
with jets of ice-cold water,
since it's you permits me to win
¯the loveliness and wisdom
which nothing can replace.

The souls of lovers open before me
in the moment of love
and I have them in my power.
Like a sculptor regarding
his work, I gaze
at their eyelid-locked faces,
tormented with ecstasy,
thickened
with joy.
Like an angel
I read the thoughts
inside their skulls.
I feel in the palm of my hand
the beating of their human hearts,
I hear the words
they whisper to each other
in life's sincerest moment.

I enter their souls
and wander
along the road of rapture or horror
to lands as unfathomed
as the ocean beds.
Then, loaded with treasures,
I return, slowly,
to myself.

Oh, so many riches,
so many priceless truths,
growing ever greater in metaphysical echo,
so much secret knowledge,

subtle and awesome,
do I owe to you, my thigh.

The most perfect beauty of soul
would give me no such treasures
were it not for your bright smooth charm;
you amoral little animal.

*Translated by Margaret Marshment
and Grazyna Baran*

Lynn Peters

WHY DOROTHY WORDSWORTH IS NOT AS FAMOUS AS HER BROTHER

'I wandered lonely as a . . .
They're in the top drawer, William,
Under your socks –
I wandered lonely as a –
No not that drawer, the top one.
I wandered by myself –
Well wear the ones you can find,
No, don't get overwrought my dear,
I'm coming.'

'I was out one day wandering
Lonely as a cloud when –
Softboiled egg, yes my dear,
As usual, three minutes –
As a cloud when all of a sudden –
Look, I said I'll cook it,
Just hold on will you –
All right, I'm coming.

'One day I was out for a walk
When I saw this flock –
It can't be too hard, it had three minutes.
Well put some butter in it.

– This host of golden daffodils
As I was out for a stroll one –

'Oh you fancy a stroll, do you.
Yes, all right William. I'm coming.
It's on the peg. Under your hat.
I'll bring my pad, shall I, in case
You want to jot something down?'

Chrystos

TOLSTOY

the great writer
        who cared so much for the poor
           they say
seduced
a virgin serving girl in his aunt's house
She was dismissed
Later he wrote a novel   His wife wrote in her diary
that he described   . . . *fornication between the serving girl*
& the officer with the peculiar
relish of a gastronome
eating something tasty
His wife   ought to know
   The serving girl probably had his child
probably died young
certainly the child died without ever learning to read or write
    or meeting his father
ALL   we know of her
is her name   Masha

  For Uta Fellechner

Patience Agbabi

RAPPIN' IT UP

I was in a bar once eyeing up the cocktails
waitin' for a friend of mine won't bore you with the details
when I hear a voice that is gettin' me annoyed it sounds like
Mind if I join you? Peace destroyed.
Waitin' for a friend, um, What's your name? Patience
Saw you coming out of the underground station
Get you a drink? No Do you come here oft . . . Yes
What d'you do? I said I am a poet ess.

Funny you should say that, fancy a quick one?
Write a bit myself ya know, get yer lips round this one:
I wandered lonely as a cloud
So I drank down my drink an' I said it out aloud:
I walked on my own from the underground station
list'ning to the beauty of my own imagination
Happy jus' being alone in my head
So don't give me a line from a poet that's dead

Coz I'm rappin' it up in a real tight squeeze
I don't cross my eyes   I don't dot my teas
Wordsworth   Milton   line them up
an' they're dead   I am PA an' I am rappin' it up.

I was at a gig once   listen to the ska–beat
jivin' and writhing an' hot with a body heat
when I feel an arm that is gettin' me annoyed
an' the hot sweaty fingers I learn to avoid. It say
Mind if I join you   really find you sexy
saw you dancin' on yer own an' thought I'd introduce me
Get you a drink? No.   Have we met before?   Yes.
What d'ya do?   I said I am a poetess.   He said

Funny you should say that   we ought to get it going
I've spent my whole life jus' writing one poem
a masterpiece,   it's called *Paradise Lost*
and the beat slowed down an' then the music stopped. I said
I skanked on my own to the ska–beat music
lovin' every minute till ya come to abuse it

grabbin' an' clawin' an' pushin' and pawin'
I don't give a shit about your master poem. Coz I'm

rappin' it up in a real tight squeeze
I don't cross my eyes   I don't dot my teas
Milton   Shakespeare   line them up
an' they're dead.   I am PA an' I am rappin' it up

I was at the disco   listen to the Hip Hop
head was a buzzin' so I thought it never would stop
along comes Shakespeare and the boys
an' it's lock up yer daughters I'm the King of Noise
He stand on the stage an' begin a recitation
A to Z of a famous quotation
not a spark originality
they ain't clappin'   they're nappin' so listen ta me
I said Get off the stage an' go home to your bed
coz I am alive an' you are dead
an' when you try to speak your words are obsolete
While I communicate right from yer head down ta yer feet
because   I'm
            rappin' it up in a real tight squeeze
I don't cross my eyes   I don't dot my teas
Shakespeare   Milton   Pope and Dryden
Wordsworth   Eliot   Great Tradition
all you poets   I don't give a fuck
coz you're dead   I am PA   an' I am

RAPPIN'
IT
UP

Sappho

HYMEN HYMENAON!

FIRST   Raise the rafters! Hoist
VOICE   them higher! Here comes

                    a bridegroom taller
                    than Ares!

SECOND   *Hymen*
VOICE   *Hymenaon!*

FIRST   He towers
VOICE   above tall men as
             poets of Lesbos
             over all others!

SECOND   *Sing Hymen*
VOICE   *O Hymenaon*

Translated by Mary Barnard

Edna St Vincent Millay

SONNET XXXI

Oh, oh, you will be sorry for that word!
Give back my book and take my kiss instead.
Was it my enemy or my friend I heard,
'What a big book for such a little head!'
Come, I will show you now my newest hat,
And you may watch me purse my mouth and prink!
Oh, I shall love you still, and all of that.
I never again shall tell you what I think.
I shall be sweet and crafty, soft and sly;
You will not catch me reading any more:
I shall be called a wife to pattern by;
And some day when you knock and push the door,
Some sane day, not too bright and not too stormy,
I shall be gone, and you may whistle for me.

Chris Mansell

DEFINITION POEM: PISSED AS A PARROT

For those of you who are etymologically inclined
I would like to take this opportunity
to explain to you the derivation of the expression
pissed as a parrot.

Sidney Baker in *The Australian Language* indexes
      Paroo dog
      Parrot
      Parson's pox
There is no entry under *pissed.* .
he also gives
      Proverbial, come the
      Piss, panther's
and   Pseudoxy.

Parrot on page 55 is a sheep
which has lost some of its wool.
If the sheep's fly-blown it's a rosella.

Wilkes in his *Dictionary of Australian Colloquialisms*
lists only to piss in someone's pocket
(refer Kylie Tennant, Bray, Hardy & Herbert)
Pissant around (Dymphna Cusack)
and Pissant, game as a.
There is no mention of any parrot in any condition at all.

In *Collins English Dictionary* (Australian edition)
you will find definitions for
      piss
      piss about
      Pissaro
      piss artist
and   piss off.

Parrots appear in their psittaciformes capacity
which I found meant having a short hooked bill,
Compact body, and an ability
to mimic.
It was not entirely clear whether this referred to birds.

Parrot-fashion had nothing to do with anything.

Roget's *Thesaurus*
Nuttal's *Dictionary of Synonyms and Antonyms*
Stillman's *Poets Manual and Rhyming Dictionary*
Webster's *Treasury of Synonyms, Antonyms and Homonyms*
and the *Shorter Oxford English Dictionary*
were no help at all.

I thought *Usage & Abusage*
being by Partridge
could be illuminating, but it appears
that neither piss nor parrots are abused.

I refused to consult Strunk's *Elements of Style*
on the grounds that the backcover blurb
has quotes from the *Greensboro Daily News*
and *The Telephone Engineers and Management Journal*.

But I went to afternoon tea
in the School of Chemistry at the University of Sydney
at 4 pm on Thursday 6 November
and there, Dr A.R. Lacey, physical chemist, MSc PhD,
informed me, in his capacity as a true blue,
down to earth, dinky-di, grass roots Aussie that
when working on his horse stud in the Wingecarribee Shire
he had observed that Gang Gang cockatoos
fall with paralytic suddenness
from the branches of Hawthorn bushes
after ingesting the berries.

Incredibly, *The Reader's Digest Complete Book of Australian Birds*
makes no mention of this.

Eunice de Souza

MY STUDENTS

My students think it funny
that Daruwallas and de Souzas
should write poetry.
Poetry is faery lands forlorn.
Women writers Miss Austen.
Only foreign men air their crotches.

Connie Bensley

FAIDAGERY

Three men in camel overcoats – coarse, moon-faced,
slicked-back hair – are sitting in the front row
of an audience.

They mutter to each other disapprovingly
then rise, button their coats
and ostentatiously leave, saying:

'I can't stand to see women committing
Faidagery.'

It's not in the dictionary: I look for it
when I wake up. But it might be in some
arcane tome or medical compendium.

One could be committing Faidagery
in all innocence.
There is always something you do
which annoys somebody.

'Listen now if you dare'

Marsha Prescod

TO BO . . .

Well shit!
Its official.
Looks like they invented it.
Our hair, I mean.

Like they invented
Pyramids
Jazz
Universities
Tap-dancing.

So,
Nows the time,
For every Black man, woman, child, dog and cat,
To pick up dey 'teach yourself Swahili' books,
And dey reggae/jazz/calypso records,
Jump in dem good ol' canoes,

An start to paddle for strictly tropical shores,
Cause,
Having invented *the whole, goddam universe,*
Looks like there's nothing left for them to invent now,
But us.

Eleanor Dare

FIVE-FINGER DISCOUNTS

'A great deal of talent is lost in this world for
want of a little courage.'

About shoplifting,
for all those who still believe
Big Daddy is watching You –
Bullshit.
Just say the shoplifters prayer:

Survive Danger
Be afraid and go on
See fear and diminish it.
There are luscious things
crying out for a woman's swift touch,
Take them!

As for store detectives
They are easily uncovered,
they look like they are at work
i.e. depressed, unimaginatively dressed.
They hold us down with fear –
An army of omniscient fathers
Ubiquitous eyes,
Surveillance cameras, their
dissapproving lenses tracking
our private minds.

Shed guilt, take more than is given and pass it on,
forget the fathers, headmasters
they all had an interest in keeping us down.
Stealing is exhilarating, ribcage acceleration
two fingers to drab minds of
primary school teachers and tedious preachers.

Besides,
the rich are unworthy of some things –
Star fruit,
Lapis Lazuli,
Beautiful books.
We are dangerous
We have ingenuity, defiance,
the righteous indignation
of a thousand years.
Laugh out loud –
all they can come up with
is the
rattle of keys.

Leonora Speyer

WITCH!

Ashes of me,
Whirl in the fires I may not name.
Lick, lovely flame!

Will the fagot not burn?
Throw on the tired broom
Stabled still in my room.

I have ridden wide and well.
Shall I say with whom?
(Stop the town bell!)

Listen now,
Listen now if you dare:
I have lain with hope
Under the dreadful bough,
I have suckled Judas' rope
As it swung on the air—

Go find the silver pieces in the moon.
I hid them there.

Vicki Raymond

THE SENDING OF FIVE

Five potent curses
I send you, the first
love, which frequently
drives men to suffer
uncouth hair transplants.

The second, riches,
bringing in their train
the envy of friends

expressed in these words:
'It's alright for some.'

My third curse is fame:
may you become sport
for reporters, may
the dull quote you, may
cranks think they *are* you.

My fourth, contentment,
hugging you, white grub,
in a fat cocoon
that the cries of men
cannot penetrate.

And last, a longlife.
May you live to be
called 'The Grand Old Man.'
Smiling at you, may
the young sprain their jaws.

Christina Walsh

A WOMAN TO HER LOVER
('*Proudly*')

Do you come to me to bend me to your will
As conqueror to the vanquished
To make of me a bondslave
To bear you children, wearing out my life
In drudgery and silence
No servant will I be
If that be what you ask, O Lover ('*ironically*') I refuse you!

('*Mockingly-drawing room ballad style*')

Or if you think to wed with one from heaven sent
Whose every deed and word and wish is golden
A wingless angel who can do no wrong

Go! – I am no doll to dress and sit for feeble worship
If that be what you ask, fool, I refuse you!

('*Slowly*')

Or if you think in me to find
A creature who will have no greater joy
Than gratify your clamorous desire,
My skin soft only for your fond caresses
My body supple only for your sense delight,
Oh shame, and pity and abasement.
Not for you the hand of any wakened woman of our time.

But Lover, if you ask of me
That I shall be your comrade, friend, and mate,
To live and work, to love and die with you,
That so together we may know the purity and height
Of passion, and of joy and sorrow,
Then O husband, I am yours forever
And our co-equal love will make the stars to laugh with joy
And we shall have the music of the spheres for bridal march
And to its circling fugue pass on, hand holding hand
Until we reach the very heart of God.

Stevie Smith

LIGHTLY BOUND

You beastly child, I wish you had miscarried,
You beastly husband, I wish I had never married.
You hear the north wind riding fast past the window? He calls me.
Do you suppose I shall stay when I can go so easily?

Margaret Atwood

IS/NOT

i

Love is not a profession
genteel or otherwise

sex is not dentistry
the slick filling of aches and cavities

you are not my doctor
you are not my cure,

nobody has that
power, you are merely a fellow/traveller.

Give up this medical concern,
buttoned, attentive,

permit yourself anger
and permit me mine

which needs neither
your approval nor your surprise

which does not need to be made legal
which is not against a disease

but against you,
which does not need to be understood

or washed or cauterized,
which needs instead

to be said and said.
Permit me the present tense.

ii

I am not a saint or a cripple,
I am not a wound; now I will see
whether I am a coward.

I dispose of my good manners,
you don't have to kiss my wrists.

This is a journey, not a war,
there is no outcome,
I renounce predictions

and aspirins, I resign the future
as I would resign an expired passport:
picture and signature are gone
along with holidays and safe returns.

We're stuck here
on this side of the border
in this country of thumbed streets and stale buildings

where there is nothing spectacular.
to see and the weather is ordinary

where *love* occurs in its pure form only
on the cheaper of the souvenirs

where we must walk slowly,
where we may not get anywhere

or anything, where we keep going,
fighting our ways, our way
not out but through.

Anon, Chinese folk

'I'M EIGHTEEN'

I'm eighteen,
he's nine.
At night
I carry him to the ivory bed.
He's more son than man.
Damn the lousy matchmaker
who found me a husband
small as a nail.

In the middle of the night
he pisses on me.

Translated by Cecilia Liang

Fleur Adcock

AGAINST COUPLING

I write in praise of the solitary act:
of not feeling a trespassing tongue
forced into one's mouth, one's breath
smothered, nipples crushed against the
ribcage, and that metallic tingling
in the chin set off by a certain odd nerve:

unpleasure. Just to avoid those eyes would help –
such eyes as a young girl draws life from,
listening to the vegetal
rustle within her, as his gaze
stirs polypal fronds in the obscure
sea-bed of her body, and her own eyes blur.

There is much to be said for abandoning
this no longer novel exercise –
for not 'participating in
a total experience' – when
one feels like the lady in Leeds who
had seen *The Sound of Music* eighty-six times;

or more, perhaps, like the school drama mistress
producing *A Midsummer Night's Dream*
for the seventh year running, with
yet another cast from 5B.
Pyramus and Thisbe are dead, but
the hole in the wall can still be troublesome.

I advise you, then, to embrace it without
encumbrance. No need to set the scene,
dress up (or undress), make speeches.

Five minutes of solitude are
enough – in the bath, or to fill
that gap between the Sunday papers and lunch.

Ana Castillo

ONE FIFTEEN

Is it possible for hours to pass so slowly,
stretching like elastic, breaking the law of
nature?

Is it possible to endure such empty hours,
huge kettles of black clay, fragile and common?

i'll be an old woman before the day ends, and the
night is worse! before dawn an eternal trip
with no destination

give me a hammer to break the clock's
cynical face, its crossed arms and that
tongue sticking out at me!

i'm going to put a bomb in the phone company
because mine doesn't ring, and i won't
pay my bill either!

i'm going to complain to god, write to the governor
give up on the president. i didn't even vote for him.

Translated from the Spanish by Carol Maier

Annie Blue

UB40 QUEUE BLUES

here come the UB40 queue blues
the dirty wall fuck it all
come to claim my due blues

here come the thursday a.m. grime time
the stand in line number nine
crazy pantomime time

here come the thirty minute hate show
you're not there deadly stare
i'm gonna make you wait show

here come the just another face race
scrounging mob aint got no job
so you'd better know your place race

here come the UB40 queue blues
the dirty wall fuck it all
come to claim my due blues

Bessie Jackson (Lucille Bogan)

STEW MEAT BLUES

A man say I had something
                    look like new
He wanted me to credit him
                    for some of my stew
Say he's going up the river
                    try to sell his sack
He would pay me for my stuff
                    when the boat get back
     Now you can go on up the river
     Man and sell your sack
     You can pay me for my stew
     When the boat get back

I got good stew
               and it's got to be sold
The price ain't high
               I want to get you told
     Go on up the river

Man and sell your sack
There'll be stew meat here
Baby when the boat get back

Now look here man
                          what you want me to do
Give you my stew meat
                          and credit you too
You go on up the river
Try and sell your sack
'Cause I have my stew meat here
When that boat get back

I credit one man
                    it was to my sorrow
It's cash today
                  credit tomorrow
So hurry up the river
Baby and try to sell your sack
It's gonna be meat here
When that boat get back

Now it's ashes to ashes
                          dust to dust
You try my stuff one time
                                you can't get enough
So go on up the river
Man and sell your sack
'Cause the stuff'll be here
Baby when the boat get back

Ann Ziety

ONE DAY HE'S GONNA COOK ME A MEAL

one day he's gonna cook me a meal
a big meal
a big monster of a meal

with perfectly roasted crispy potatoes
and succulent garden-grown baby carrots
nesting like sneaky little surprises
beneath some richly flavoured sauce

one day he's gonna cook me a meal
and for once his timing will be perfect

he will go to all that trouble
of scraping and slicing and peeling and dicing
of reaching boiling point
and taking care not to burn
and taking time over all those little details
and stirring and blending and caring and worrying
breaking down over the creme caramel
but not wanting any help or instructions
and never, no never
giving up and instead making pilchard sandwiches
with stale bread

he will arrange everything
like an exuberant Egon Ronay
on a willow-pattern dinner plate
swirling with dancing tongues of curling steam
and offer it to me like some long lost treasure

and I'm not going to say thank you
I'm not going to say aren't you having some
I will eat it, insatiable
sucking it up like an empty whale
my head stuck right in there
cramming my mouth with a vegetable paradise
grunting over the creamy white horseradish
gobbling like some hysterical piglet
slopping it everywhere
my face mottled with dark ripples of gravy
which run unstoppable down my chin
my neck my breasts
and congeal
in a brown solid stain
right where my heart is

one day he's gonna cook me a meal
and I'm gonna run my hands through it
feel the squelch of steaming mash
squeeze those pretty little peas till they pop
cram my ears full of pulpy swede
burrow into the thick nest of buttered cabbage
gorge and wallow and swim around
in the sweet-smelling juices
till the cows come home
till I burst with greed
till I can't breathe any more

I'll probably die
but it'll be worth it
cos hell
I've been waiting for this meal
a long time

Wisława Szymborska

THE WOMEN OF RUBENS

Giantesses, female fauna,
naked as the rumbling of barrels.
They sprawl in trampled beds,
sleep with mouths agape for crowing.
Their eyes have fled into the depths
and penetrate to the very core of glands
from which yeast seeps into the blood.

Daughters of the Baroque. Dough rises in kneading-troughs,
baths are asteam, wines glow ruby,
piglets of cloud gallop across the sky,
trumpets neigh an alert of the flesh.

O meloned, O excessive ones,
doubled by the flinging off of shifts,
trebled by the violence of posture,
you lavish dishes of love!

Their slender sisters had risen earlier,
before dawn broke in the picture.
No one noticed how, single file, they
had moved to the canvas's unpainted side.

Exiles of style. Their ribs all showing,
their feet and hands of birdlike nature.
Trying to take wing on bony shoulder blades.

The thirteenth century would have given them a golden
    background,
the twentieth – a silver screen.
The seventeenth had nothing for the flat of chest.

For even the sky is convex,
convex the angels and convex the god –
mustachioed Phoebus who on a sweaty
mount rides into the seething alcove.

Translated by Magnus J. Krynski and Robert A. Maguire

Dilys Bennett Laing

OCEAN FABLE

There is a fish
whose anus is his mouth.
In his beginning is his end.
He is his own foe and friend

and the reply to his own wish.
This creature of primeval mud
is born forever in the blood.
But higher up, in swifter tides,

the murderous swordfish stabs and slides.
They say the complex octopus

is subtly brained and amorous.
I, tidal in my acts and wishes,

perceive how hierarchies of fishes
kill and make love in me. My God,

grant me the rage of shark or cod
but mark my exits, one for dung,

another for the mind and tongue,
and let the fish whose shape is O
cease breeding self in night below.

Caroline Claxton

LESBIAN

YOUR IMAGE:
I am a lesbian
I open cans with my teeth.
I have a domineering mother,
except when I have a domineering father,
sister, brother, school-friend, neighbour, gay man who came to
   read the gas meter
when I was six.
I creep out
at the dead of night
to steal men's underpants
which I wear – under my tweed skirt.
I live at Greenham
except when I live next door to you.
I go to drop-in centres
for left-wing-commie-cigar-smoking-butch-bulldykes-against-
   the-bomb
paid for by the GLC.
I have fourteen fingers
we grow extra ones
you know.
I leap out from under 'man'hole covers
to grab 'straight' women
And I'm secretly plotting with Russia

to 'dis–arm' Ronald Reagan.

HOW IT IS:
You've never quite got it right
about me
So let me tell you about myself.

I am complicated but
surprisingly average.
I do everything
and as for jobs:
I have a good job, a bad job, no job
I'm fired from jobs, I create jobs
I've worked just about any kind of job you can think of
except Prime Minister
unfortunately.

I am a thousand colours
and come from a thousand places
I come in a thousand places
and out in a thousand places.

I am behind you in the bus queue,
the cinema, the supermarket.
I live everywhere
except Buckingham Palace
as far as I know.

I am older than spoken word
traces of my bones lie in the stones
beneath your feet.
I am made of rock
harder than diamond
It cuts through your conventions
and your sticky, sticky lies.

I am more women than you would believe
And more woman than you would understand.

What am I?

Dorothy Parker

NEITHER BLOODY NOR BOWED

They say of me, and so they should
It's doubtful if I come to good.
I see acquaintances and friends
Accumulating dividends,
And making enviable names
In science, art and parlour games.
But I, despite expert advice,
Keep doing things I think are nice,
And though to good I never come –
Inseparable my nose and thumb!

Bridget Jones

THERMO-STATIC

Last night was
Hot hot
Braided your body hair
Right down
Sucked your left toe
Right off
My sweet lies
Your matt eyes
Our wet sweat gleaming

Then sleep
thick
as red pea soup
knotted with dumpling

Today
We pass
By Barclay's Bank
Your left lid flickers
I crook a digit

Cool cool.

Debra Bruce

HEY BABY

Some men can strip
a woman down, while
they put a building up.
A whistle, a look—

One hoot from him as he dangles
from a moving crane, and off
go my clothes, and I am all ass,
ass, flaring with every step.
My body gets so hot so fast
it burns the air everywhere
with shapes of me but only he
can see them.

Chances are there's nothing hard
on him but his hat. Still,
what I feel makes my nipples burn,
and not with lust, or love.

a–dZiko Simba

TIME AND PLACE

Sugar,
If you are passing in your car –
In the opposite direction
and you notice my silk black legs
        my provocative hips and
    the sunshine in my eyes,
and the mood takes you to –
comment
on my loveliness –
of course I will flirt and wave
behaving like you are my only true love.

I will shoot kisses through the air
and share
this fleeting intimacy.
If
you are passing
In your car –
in the opposite
direction.

But –
If it's late.
If I have missed the last bus
and, in desperation
I am rabbit-darting home
If it's dark
and
cold
and there's dampness in the air
and the ghosts of the day just passed
whisper warnings.
If you come driving by,
Aretha Franklin in your ears
protected by the
warmth and speed of –
your metal love
If you
see me
and opportunity springs to mind . . .

don't stop mister
just don't stop.

Anon, Chinese folk

'WATER BUCKETS SWING'

Water buckets swing
from her shoulders.
'Hey, girl,
your bucket's got a leak.
Stand still
and let me plug the hole
so the water
won't wet your feet.'

'I shoulder my water
and my buckets swing.
My bucket's got no leak.
If there's a hole
I've got a man to plug it.'

Translated by Cecilia Liang

Nina Cassian

LADY OF MIRACLES

Since you walked out on me
I'm getting lovelier by the hour.
I glow like a corpse in the dark.
No one sees how round and sharp
my eyes have grown
how my carcass looks like a glass urn,
how I hold up things in the rags of my hands,
the way I can stand though crippled by lust.
No, there's just your cruelty circling
my head like a bright rotting halo.

Translated by Brenda Walker and Andrea Deletant

Margaret Atwood

SIREN SONG

This is the one song everyone
would like to learn: the song
that is irresistible:

the song that forces men
to leap overboard in squadrons
even though they see the beached skulls

the song nobody knows
because anyone who has heard it
is dead, and the others can't remember.

Shall I tell you the secret
and if I do, will you get me
out of this bird suit?

I don't enjoy it here
squatting on this island
looking picturesque and mythical

with these two feathery maniacs,
I don't enjoy singing
this trio, fatal and valuable.

I will tell the secret to you,
to you, only to you.
Come closer. This song

is a cry for help: Help me!
Only you, only you can,
you are unique

at last. Alas
it is a boring song
but it works every time.

Mary Elizabeth Coleridge

THE WITCH

I have walked a great while over the snow,
And I am not tall nor strong.
My clothes are wet, and my teeth are set,
And the way was hard and long.
I have wandered over the fruitful earth,
But I never came here before.
Oh, lift me over the threshold, and let me in
        at the door!

The cutting wind is a cruel foe.
I dare not stand in the blast.
My hands are stone, and my voice a groan,

and the worst of death is past.
I am but a little maiden still,
My little white feet are sore.
Oh, lift me over the threshold, and let me in
        at the door!

Her voice was the voice that women have,
Who plead for their heart's desire.
She came – she came – and the quivering flame
Sank and died in the fire.
It never was lit again on my hearth
Since I hurried across the floor,
To lift her over the threshold, and let her in
        at the door!

Fiona Pitt-Kethley

COUNTRY WALK

I went into the countryside for a walk
and took some bread for the ducks
and my camera to take photographs.

As I carefully shut the farm gate
the old bull said 'Leave that open
Missus, I want to see that
heifer next door – last time she
had a headache.'
I went to the pond and threw bread to the ducks –
'Stuff your Mother's Pride' they said,
'We wants worms.'
I put up my camera to take a picture of a nest,
and the birds said 'God damn that voyeur,
let's crap on her lenses.'
I sat down for my picnic.
There was a little hedgehog nearby,
I undid my thermos and poured him some milk.
And the hedgehog said, 'Keep your filthy
cow-muck, I haven't got stomach ulcers.
What I want is your pin-cushion for a dildo.'

Ann Dancy

PARTY

Pearl's at the table, hefting a big knife,
giving the cucumber what-for, hammering
the handle straight down to the board, singing.
The kitchen's clean, every surface covered
with food, cans, bottles; every surface shines
and we are settled, domestic as cats.
Certainly the hottest day this year
but she keeps the multi-coloured jacket on,
rolls up her sleeves and cools herself on lager.

Knock it back. We're celebrating too soon.
These cans sound empty, and, with hours to go
we should be measuring the whisky.
I check the oven, slosh water round the sink,
worry about the garden, open cupboards

and shut them, forgetting. She fills a glass.
I shuffle an ashtray of ring-pulls. I want
to sleep, to have another drink. I want to stop.
You can't have everything, she says, Sup up.

When I come back from the phone, she's dancing;
the radio's retuned, turned up. I'm moving
despite myself, despite the lack of space.
Cards waver as we pass. Love, more love,
jokes, All my love. Some fall. 'I'm 39.'
I say, trying it out. Well done, she says,
and holds me closer, patting my shoulder
like a mother. My face is hot, I'm wondering
about opening windows, about falling out.

Tell tale tit your tongue will split
but this is my friend. I'll tell half.
She lights a cigarette, squints
to place it in my mouth, picks up a glass
closes my fingers on it. 'A man.
That's all. I'll be alright.' Strikes me, she says,
It's going to your head. Just sober up.
It's not too late. He's irresistible
but so's a finger down the throat.

Sappho

'YES, IT IS PRETTY'

Yes, it is pretty

But come, dear, need
you pride yourself
that much on a ring?

Translated by Mary Barnard

Suniti Namjoshi

CONTEMPORARY

The government official
speaks in English with friends,
in Hindi with servants,
and reserves his mother tongue
for his 2 Alsatian dogs.

Meiling Jin

I GET AROUND

Do i remind you of
someone else
who was a nurse?

a nice girl

Did you see me
on TV, you know
what's that programme called?

Have you met
my sister Kay?
She's just like me
she's studying to be

a nurse.

i'm sure
you might have seen me
somewhere:
serving you,
or nursing you,
or cleaning up
your rubbish.

Yes madam,
we *do* look alike

and we even eat dogs
where i come from.

Anon

POEM FROM HOLLOWAY PRISON, 1912

There was a small woman called G,
Who smashed two big windows at B—
They sent her to jail, her fate to bewail,
For Votes must be kept, must be kept for the male.

They asked that small woman called G,
Why she smashed those big windows at B—
She made a long speech, then made her defence,

But it wasn't no use, their heads were so dense;
They just hummed the refrain, altho' it is stale—
Votes must be kept, must be kept for the male.

They sent her to H for six months and a day,
In the coach Black Maria she went sadly away;
But she sang in this strain, as it jolted and rumbled,
We will have the Vote, we will not be humbled.
We must have the vote by hill and by dale,
Votes shall not alone be kept for the male.

C. M. Donald

OUT

The corset had
hooks and eyes
marking the flesh
under the zip
so it could be closed.

It reduced
sensation in the stomach,
and circulation
in the shoulders and,
of course, movement.

It wasn't any good,
was it? You
meant it for the best,
I know, but it
didn't keep me in.

I'm out of bounds,
out of breath,
out of sight,
outfront and
out of the closet
and what was it, actually,
that needed to be under control?

Anon, 1920

DOWN IN NEW ORLEANS

When I was a servant girl way down in New Orleans,
My master was a king and my mistress was a queen;
And there I met a sailor from far across the sea,
And he's the son-of-a-bitch who started all my misery.
He asked me for a candle to light his way to bed,
He asked me for a handkerchief to tie around his head;
For I was young and pure and thought it was no harm
And I jumped into his bed to keep the sailor warm.
Next morning very early when I at last awoke
The sailor blithely handed me a dollar note.
Now all fair maidens please do take a tip from me:
Never let a sailor go an inch above your knee;
For I tried once and once is more than enough for me
The bastard left me with a dose of gonorrhea.

'*The bush catches fire*'

Nikki Giovanni

SEDUCTION

one day
you gonna walk in this house
and i'm gonna have on a long African
gown
you'll sit down and say 'The Black . . .'
and i'm gonna take one arm out
then you – not noticing me at all – will say 'What about
this brother . . .'
and i'm going to be slipping it over my head
and you'll rap on about 'The revolution . . .'
while i rest your hand against my stomach
you'll go on – as you always do – saying
'I just can't dig . . .'
while i'm moving your hand up and down
and i'll be taking your dashiki off
then you'll say 'What we really need . . .'
and i'll be licking your arm
and 'The way I see it we ought to . . .'
and unbuckling your pants
'And what about the situation . . .'
and taking your shorts off
then you'll notice
your state of undress
and knowing you you'll just say
'Nikki,
isn't this counterrevolutionary . . .?'

Izumi Shikibu

'A DIVER DOES NOT ABANDON'

A diver does not abandon
a seaweed filled bay . . .
Will you then turn away

from this floating, sea–foam body
that waits for your gathering hands?

Translated by Jane Hirshfield with
Mariko Aratani

Mary Webb

THUNDERBOLTS★

Stretched at harvesters' ease we lay,
Burnt nigh black, where the poppies thickened,
Never a thing had we to say,
Thunder rolled in the hills all day.

My shirt was torn and I reeked of sweat;
All my body was blazing and quickened.
She was untidy and sulky, yet
Something about her you couldn't forget.

I got my knife and began to hack
Elder whistles to keep me quiet.
'Jim', she said, as she lay there slack,
'I won't go on, and we can't go back.'

I asked what she meant, but I knew. The sight
Of her scornful look made my blood go riot,
I showed her a poppy, straight and bright,
Crushed in my hand: we stilled at the sight.

Thunder broke on the hills at night.

★ *Scarlet poppies are called thunderbolts in*
Shropshire.

Sujata Bhatt

SHÉRDI*

The way I learned,
to eat sugar cane in Sanosra:
I use my teeth
to tear the outer hard *chaal*
then, bite off strips
of the white fibrous heart –
suck hard with my teeth, press down
and the juice spills out.

January mornings
the farmer cuts tender green sugar cane
and brings it to our door.
Afternoons, when the elders are asleep
we sneak outside carrying the long smooth stalks.
The sun warms us, the dogs yawn,
our teeth grow strong
our jaws are numb;
for hours we suck out the *russ,* the juice
                              sticky all over our hand

So tonight
when you tell me to use my teeth,
to suck hard, harder,
then, I smell sugar cane grass
                    in your hair
and imagine you'd like to be
shérdi   shérdi   out in the fields
          the stalks sway
                    opening a path before us

★ *(Shérdi): sugar cane*

Anon

LOVE'S POWER

'O Sir,' quoth the pretty maid,
     'Let me know what 'tis you would have?
For you need not at all be afraid,
     I will grant what in reason you crave:
For I ne'er in my life would deny
     What a man did in justice require;
But you and I soon shall comply,
     And I'll warrant I'll quench thy love's fire.'

'If thou art so earnest do dally,
     Come make use of time while you may,
Thy skill I will not undervalue,
     Then prithee, Love, let's to the play:
Methinks thou art somewhat too devious;
     'Tis time we should have been nigher,
To linger it seems to be grevious,
     I'll warrant I'll quench thy love's fire.'

The young man supposing her greedy
     Fell eagerly into the sport,
He found she was wanting and needy,
     And needless it was for to court.
But as they were hugging together,
     She cried, 'O come nigher and nigher.'
His heart was as light as a feather,
     And he had both his wish and desire.
The damsel was mightily pleased,
     And kissed him a thousand times o'er,
Quoth she, 'Now my sorrows are eased,
     But I must have a little touch more:
O, lie down for a while to rest thee,
     That I may enjoy my desire;
I hope that the fates they will bless thee;
     I quench, but thou kindlest my fire.'

No longer he stood there delaying,
     But stoutly he fell to it again,

Where he gave a prod at their playing
  The damsel returned him ten;
For she grew more eager and eager,
  Her eyes they did sparkle like fire,
Quoth he, 'I do own I am the weaker,
  But still I enjoy my desire.'

The young man began for to tire
  And his cudgel began to lay down,
Which made the young damsel admire
  And straight she began for to frown:
Quoth he, 'I have done what is fit,
  No reason can more require';
But her brows upon her then she knit,
  And still she did want her desire.

Carol Ann Duffy

OPPENHEIM'S CUP AND SAUCER

She asked me to luncheon in fur. Far from
the loud laughter of men, our secret life stirred.

I remember her eyes, the slim rope of her spine.
This is your cup, she whispered, and this mine.

We drank the sweet hot liquid and talked dirty.
As she undressed me, her breasts were a mirror

and there were mirrors in the bed. She said Place
your legs around my neck, that's right. Yes.

Anon, Chinese folk

'YOU'RE LIKE BAMBOO'

You're like bamboo
shooting out of the ground.
I'm the bamboo husk
and I'll wrap you
until the end of spring.

Translated by Cecilia Liang

Aphra Behn

SONG: THE WILLING MISTRISS

Amyntas led me to a Grove,
   Where all the Trees did shade us;
The Sun it self, though it had Strove,
   It could not have betray'd us:

The place secur'd from humane Eyes,
   No other fear allows,
   But when the Winds that gently rise,
Doe Kiss the yeilding Boughs.

Down there we satt upon the Moss,
   And did begin to play
A Thousand Amorous Tricks, to pass
   The heat of all the day.
A many Kisses he did give:
   And I return'd the same
Which made me willing to receive
   That which I dare not name.

His Charming Eyes no Aid requir'd
   To tell their softning Tale;
On her that was already fir'd,
   'Twas Easy to prevaile.
He did but Kiss and Clasp me round,

Whilst those his thoughts Exprest:
And lay'd me gently on the Ground;
Ah who can guess the rest?

Anon, 12th century AD

'I LIKE SLEEPING WITH SOMEBODY'

I like sleeping with somebody
different

often

It's nicest when my husband is
in a foreign country

and there's rain in the streets at night
and wind

and nobody

Translated from the Sanskrit by Willis Barnstone

Anna Wickham

THE FIRED POT

In our town, people live in rows.
The only irregular thing in a street is the steeple;
And where that points to God only knows,
And not the poor disciplined people!

And I have watched the women growing old,
Passionate about pins, and pence, and soap,
Till the heart within my wedded breast grew cold,
And I lost hope.

But a young soldier came to our town,
He spoke his mind most candidly.

He asked me quickly to lie down,
And that was very good for me.

For though I gave him no embrace –
Remembering my duty –
He altered the expression of my face,
And gave me back my beauty.

Ono no Komachi

'IF, IN AN AUTUMN FIELD'

If, in an autumn field,
a hundred flowers
can untie their streamers,
may I not also openly frolic,
as fearless of blame?

*Translated by Jane Hirshfield with
Mariko Aratani*

Susan Kelly

BLIND CUPID

'Do you like older women?' I asked, rather coy.
(For myself, I confess, I could use a toy boy).
'A charming arrangement, September and May;
Let's seal it with dinner? No problem, I'll pay.'

For a young man's a beauty, so firm and so fresh,
No widening of girth and no sagging of flesh.
No *'Where are my slippers?'* or *'Please, not tonight.'*
His chin is not twinning, his eyes are still bright.

*Yes, give me a woman of uncertain years,
No cloying, no clinging; no moping, no tears.*

No 'Don't you still love me?' *or* 'Was I okay?'
Or 'What are you thinking?' *or* 'What did I say?'

His hair's not receding, nor yet going grey;
He's virile and eager, and ready for play.
So waste no more time, let's get on, misbehave;
I'll happily make you, you sweet thing, my slave.

A nice steady income, a smart central flat,
The house in the Cotswolds? Yes, I'll drink to that.
A woman of mystery, not a young minx;
A charming enigma, a right little Sphinx.

Oh yes, I like young men, I like their firm thighs;
The power in their biceps, the light in their eyes.
Jowls that aren't drooping and ribs you can feel,
Enough shilly-shallying, is it a deal?

I need some protection, an orphan like me,
Fatherless, motherless – cruel destiny.
Yes, I like older women, especially in bed,
'What was the name, dear?' 'Jocasta,' I said.

Grace Nichols

MY BLACK TRIANGLE

My black triangle
sandwiched between the geography of my thighs

is a bermuda
of tiny atoms
forever seizing
and releasing
the world

My black triangle
is so rich
that it flows over

on to the dry crotch
of the world

My black triangle
is black light
sitting on the threshold
of the world

overlooking my deep-pink
probabilities

and though
it spares a thought
for history
my black triangle
has spread beyond his story
beyond the dry fears of parch-ri-archy

spreading and growing
trusting and flowering
my black triangle
carries the seal of approval
of my deepest self

Suniti Namjoshi

I GIVE HER THE ROSE

I give her the rose with unfurled petals.
She smiles
        and crosses her legs.
I give her the shell with the swollen lip.
She laughs. I bite
        and nuzzle her breasts.
I tell her, 'Feed me on flowers
        with wide open mouths,'
and slowly,
        she pulls down my head.

Emily Dickinson

WILD NIGHTS – WILD NIGHTS!

Wild Nights – Wild Nights!
Were I with thee
Wild Nights should be
Our luxury!

Futile – the Winds –
To a Heart in port –
Done with the Compass –
Done with the Chart!

Rowing in Eden –
Ah, the Sea!
Might I but moor – Tonight –
In Thee!

Janet Fisher

JOURNEY'S END

Getting up at half six
I drove off for Dewsbury in the fog
having had two slices of toast and
difficulty in getting my child to nursery.

Negotiating the middle lane in an
ever increasing sense of insecurity
I was hemmed in by an articulated lorry
carrying car axles from Düsseldorf to Newcastle,

causing me unfortunately to miss my junction
so that, abandoned in a stream of traffic,
I hopefully flashed my lights at the XR3i in front and,
he having returned my signal, drew in at the nearest service station.

Needing a shoulder to cry on I sat with him
on a grassy bank overlooking the Happy Eater and when

he put his hand up my skirt and nibbled my ear
life had never been sweeter.

Having renegotiated the carriageway upon
which as it happened the traffic was now thinning out
I found it by a judicious use of the accelerator
possible to get to work only twenty-seven minutes late.

Izumi Shikibu

'UNDISTURBED'

Undisturbed,
my garden fills
with summer growth –
how I wish for one
who would push the deep grass aside.

*Translated by Jane Hirshfield with
Mariko Aratani*

Alison Fell

STRIPPING BLACKCURRANTS

On a garden rug tinged with amber
your bare skin
grows a red fur.
Half a lilac leaf
sticks to your belly.

Stripping blackcurrants, the berries
split
and stain my fingers
as the stalks
tear from the fruit.

I have a yellow mane which crackles
and brown breasts
freckled as eggs.

Pushing among the leaves, I imagine
their feather fingers
as deft as yours.

Your body haunts the corner
of my eye:
books, papers, your bent head.
I want you in heat,
sticky as blackcurrants.

Deep in the tang of the bush
I remember the taste of your ear.
How you angled your neck
to offer it.

I flaunt my golden back.
It glows from within, a raging aura.
Unbelievable, how you resist me.

You read.
The bush catches fire.

Jane Barnes

BLOOMING

I wish you could be here to see my amaryllis
bloom   the first bulb I ever grew   the
first plant I ever had with an exotic name
the kind you want to say   How am I supposed to
know what that is?   Right now it's just
this single fat green spear like one
asparagus   you remember those asparagus jokes
I'm sure   you'd probably say   get that little

boy weewee out of here and then I'd say back
so refined   but that's my amaryllis   soon to be
a big red trumpet   or do I mean strumpet
you know just like if I bought a femmy red
dress with ruffles   flashy and loud and then
the amaryllis blooms   I bloom and you bloom
coming back and lifting up my skirt just in time

Anna Swir

LOVE DIVIDES THE LOVERS

You're jealous
of the joy you give me,
because I betray you
with it.
What you give me as a trickle
explodes in me
as a river.

It lifts me up
far beyond your reach,
to paradises
you will never know
and never understand.

We are foreigners, enemies,
singing our love songs
in different languages.
Your body's no more than an instrument
for giving joy
to my body,
which is much the more
chivalrous arrangement.

I won't be submerged in you.
I want you to be submerged
in me.

My laughing egoism
defends and adorns my nakedness,
it's a lifebelt.

The skin divides two beating hearts,
the love divides the lovers.
The beautiful song of the night
is a song of war.

> *Translated by Margaret Marshment and
> Grazyna Baran*

Tzu Yeh

THREE TZU YEH SONGS

It is night again
I let down my silken hair
Over my shoulders
And open my thighs
Over my lover.
'Tell me, is there any part of me
That is not lovable?'

I had not fastened my sash over my gown,
When you asked me to look out the window.
If my skirt fluttered open,
Blame the Spring wind.

The bare branches tremble
In the sudden breeze.
The twilight deepens.
My lover loves me,
And I am proud of my young beauty.

> *Translated by Kenneth Rexroth
> and L. Chung*

Rosemary Norman

SALINE

Drip, drip. The old girl's
skinny, her bones laid out
as flat as fossils, under
the sweaty blanket.
Her hair's shrivelled back
from brow and eyeholes.
Her gums chew on rough breath.
Soon she'll be dead.

And it's him, in the dim
drift of mist, her old
boy, her dear, her darling
coming for her, cock first,
bless him, as ever.
She melts, runs like summer
butter. It's good, so good, oh
yes. This is heaven.

Grace Nichols

GREASE

Grease steals in like a lover
over the body of my oven.
Grease kisses the knobs
of my stove.
Grease plays with the small
hands of my spoons.
Grease caresses the skin
of my table-cloth,
Getting into my every crease.
Grease reassures me that life
is naturally sticky.

Grease is obviously having an affair with me.

Jean Binta Breeze

DUBWISE

'cool an
    deadly'
snake
  lady
writhing
   'roun
de worlie'
  wraps
  her sinews
roun his
   pulse
  and grinds
  his pleasure
  and disgust
   into a
   one dance
  stand

to equalise
   he grins
    cockwise
    at his bredrin
  and rides
   a 'horseman scabie'
 or bubbles a
   'water
    bumpie'
   into action

the d.j.
   eases a
    spliff
  from his lyrical
   lips
  and smilingly
   orders
  'Cease'

Faye Kicknosway

GRACIE

I mean, I'm a no shoes hillbilly an' home
is deeper in the map than Kentucky or Tennessee an'
all I been raised to do is walk the chicken
yard; spillin' grain from ma's
apron, maybe once a week wear a bonnet
into town. I have red hair an' white skin;

men lean on their elbows lookin' at me. Ma's
voice tells me, 'Don't breathe so deep,' an'
the preacher says how happy I'll be when I'm dead. Skin
touchin' skin is evil. I'm to keep inside the chicken
yard, no eye's to see beneath my bonnet.
Farm boys suck their cheeks an' call, 'Come home

with me, I'll give you your own chicken
yard an' take you proudly once a week to town.' Home
ain't enough. As I spill grain from ma's
apron, I see city streets hung with lights an'
a dark room with a window lookin' on the bonnet
of the sky. Voices stroke at my skin

through its walls. When the grain's gone from ma's
apron, I hang it on its hook by her bonnet.
I figure to be my own fare North an' leave home.
My legs are crossed under a counter. I smell chicken
fry. A man leans on his elbows; his eyes drink my skin.
In a dark room, my dress undoes my body an'

I lie with him. His hot mouth comes home
on mine. I expect to hear the preacher's or ma's

voice yellin' at me, but the only voices in the wall's
                              skin
are strange an' soft. I have beer an' chicken
for breakfast. All day I wear his body like a bonnet.
My stockins are run. The streets are hung with lights an'
he sleeps. I stand by the window an'
look into the night's skin, fancy home an' the chicken
yard, ma's apron an' my head cool in its bonnet.

Helen Watson White

RED HOT POKERS

You are too much:
prickly pistons
flaming flamingoes
a sight to make for sore eyes

Upright men!
you rack the senses for an
oversight – just as to prove
a fallacy they used to treat
the witches into coal

Pokers, you are unnecessarily
poignant in your picketing

If all you want is to persuade
me you are – let alone red
or hot – don't worry
in that get-up I couldn't mistake. If you were olive
green and stone cold
sober I would have
reluctantly to take
your point

Izumi Shikibu

'DON'T BLUSH!'
*Sent when returning a purple robe that a
certain person had left behind*

Don't blush!
People will guess
that we slept
beneath the folds
of this purple-root rubbed cloth.

> *Translated by Jane Hirshfield with
> Mariko Aratani*

Julia Lee

COME ON OVER

Come on over darling,
but please don't come too soon.
We've got a date at eight
and it's only afternoon.

The way you rush me –
it ain't right.
I know you just
can't wait for tonight!
Remember love's like a
mashed p'tater
when you eat it up now
you won't have it later . . .

Come on over,
but please don't come too soon.

Impatient daddy
I know how much you care.
Impatient daddy
I know how much you care.
So poppa just take time
'cause there's lots of it to spare.

You got 'bout five, or six hours to kill?
Try runnin' up and down that same old hill.
You know you tried wrestlin',
you had too many falls?
Get a grip on your bat –
and smack a few balls.
Come on over,
but please don't come too soon.

You gotta let your sweetmeat
cook a long long time.
You gotta let your sweetmeat
cook a long long time.
You got to let it cook
if you want it to taste real fine.

You're going too fast
you better take care
you might have a flat
and you ain't got no spare!
Save all your lovin',
conserve all your power,
if that doesn't work,
then take a cold shower . . .

Come on over,
but please don't come too soon.

Bernadette Matthews

LABIA

Loot, and marked stranger
pressed in hand
deeper sort of mystery
than all the heavens sang.

labia,
sweet pressure of the female,
man's undoing
poor man

let the sweet liquid flow
soft, warm
wonderful.

labia
bloom

ah. those memories
of caressing hands
whispering sweet nothings
in my ear

climax and kiss
tell all.

loosen up crease marks
and genital flushes

labia
sorter of mice from men
cuddle a virgin
drink in
a cocktail of sperm

tighten and grip
and suck
the straddling wealth

of a nation
all its young men
are worthwhile to you.

labia,
generous juice
lump well on your cause
of hard excitement
and slake
the thirst
the thirst
of your enormous well

more precious than gold
hotter than fire
spanking and sparking
pronounced
absolutely flavoursome
and wholesome

drink up your caution of hell.

pour it out.
the thirst of your juices
ah.

save me from dues
or the parties price
for a good night

a wealth of savage red anger
a thirst in your throat
for the power in your bolt

a nice easy dress
a bawl of children
a matronly bloom

o labia, never let me get old
I want to fuck forever

for a hot backside
a ruinous old dose
of the pox.

labia,
tender extractor of all
everything lifegiving
courageous
and purposeful

scent the hot bloom of your call.

ride out the sweet nights
masterful sons and lovers
ride out the hot nights.

labia,
when you paddled the basin
and creased the inside
of even the pants of the well to do

be savage with them,
count the quick profits and run for your life
and another steamy night

it was fun
it was fun
thank you darling
and kiss him on the ear
it was delicious
and you were marvellous
and think about

anything else that could give you
a morsel of thrill.
or help you keep on
living

forever and ever

excited and delighted

Up labia,
and dance
on dear homily people
kind caring men

all prostrate
exhausted before you can say
thats better
or improving
not so slow anyhow
almost good
nearly there
yes
yes
Yes.

count the bright profits
be gentle and tease just a little
for the masterful stroke
to be right in
and in the right place at the right time.

o lump of satisfaction
of solid throat
o gilded one
how strongly packed and amazing you are.

labia,
lip of entertaining gossip
an instrument of god
a confessional
soft, sweet, easy
courted by the cunning tongue

o labia

never remorseful
always solemn as you unveil
that tempramental, swollen
deliberate and well
come.

labia
lip of the vulva
a vociferous mouth
be satisfied.

'Queens of the underworld'

Nurunnessa Choudhury

I SEE CLEOPATRA

The working girl: child-carrying, sensual.
When I look at her, I see Cleopatra.
Cleopatra – my Cleopatra.
Your twin marriage
to immature children
made you a courtisan in the world's eyes.
Cleopatra – my Cleopatra:
You never had a house of your own,
never had shelter
in strong arms and chest,
deep like the jungle
where the baby deer can hide –
you only had
a suffering crown
of thorns – only a Queen,
by greedy and carnal Caesars
you were disrobed.

My unprotected Cleopatra –
the green god gave you love,
but could not give you shelter.
The refinement of your naked beauty
took away Mark Antony's courage.

Loving Cleopatra: eternal mother:
Venus, Aphrodite: My Cleopatra!

Always like the cat
who delivers her own litter,
and carries her offspring in her mouth:
Every moment of your life spent in seeking shelter.

You sacrificed yourself proudly.
Your weapon was simply
The original and ultimate one:
And you were a solitary soldier.
Your pleasure ship, your
erotic movements were

your weapons of war.
The cry of victory in Octavius' wheels
will be extinguished, every time
he comes before your wound.
My Venus, Aphrodite, Cleopatra:
Your life was scandalous, dazzling: Undefeated!

Translated by Nurunnessa Choudhury and Paul Joseph Thomson

Cicely Herbert

LOOKING BACK

Lovely legs she had your Mam,
lovely legs! Mind,
your aunty's legs were lovely too.
They all had lovely legs.

Your uncle, his legs were lovely and all.
He used to wear a little kilt
and there were his little legs.
Thin, his were, mind. Thin little legs.

But she was stubborn your Mam
what a stubborn little madam!
She was the most
stubborn lass I ever knew.

You've got lovely legs and all.
Just like your Mam's. Mind,
I'd no time for your Mam
she was a madam when she was a lass.

Your aunty was my favourite. What a picture!
Off to school with her little satchel,
polished shoes and her little white socks.
What a picture she made.

But your Mam. I never got on with your Mam.
Dirty, she was, very dirty – and cheeky!

What a monkey, what a bitch.
I never got on with that bitch.

I made her suffer for it
little bitch, little madam
Mind, she had lovely legs, your Mam
but she was a proper bitch.

Lovely legs. Really lovely little legs.

Susan Kelly

BEHIND THE RED SHUTTERS

(*In the Spanish town of Calanda, as part of the Easter
festival, drums play throughout the night on Good Friday*)

In red-shuttered houses the down-at-heel whores
Retire to the *salon* to sharpen their claws.
Their clients, this Friday, are all out of doors
Where the drums of Calanda beat without pause.

All Andalucia is out in the street
(Where middle-class charm is forever discreet)
And the wives are all there to ensure they don't cheat
And the drums of Calanda? They don't miss a beat.

So business is bad for our ladies of pleasure
Who find, over Easter, they're ladies of leisure.
A moment of peace which they really should treasure
As the drums of Calanda still beat out their measure.

Refreshments are passed round with frequent guffaws
And the room is resplendent with squawking macaws
And their one timid customer quickly . . . withdraws
To the sound of the drums which go on without pause.

And the party grows wild with the fading of light,
And the ladies are (not to be delicate) 'tight'.

And the *salon* is throbbing with Sapphic delight
As the hearts of the ladies drum through the night.

Lorna Goodison

SHE WALKS INTO ROOMS

She walks into rooms
and they run for towels
say 'girl, dry yourself.'
And she says no, it's only light
playing upon my water-wave taffetta
dress
But her host put his hand to her face
and it came away wet.
Sometimes at nights
she has to change the sheets,
her favourite brown roses
on a lavender trellis
grow sodden
and that water has salt
in it
and that's no good for roses.
He left her all this water
to hold in the purple throat
of a flower
it overflowed onto the floors
and her silver shoes sailed
like moon-boats in it.
The water took all the curl
from her hair
It runs slick to her shoulders
where his hands spread
tributaries of rivers.
as he left he said
'It is time to learn to swim.'

So saying, he departed to a dry place
carrying silver in his hair
and deep currents in his slightest
motion.
She could have died of cold waiting
in the wet he left there
But she grew full of mysteries
like the ocean.

Adelaide Crapsey

THE WITCH

When I was a girl by Nilus stream
  I watched the desert stars arise;
My lover, he who dreamed the Sphinx,
  Learned all his dreaming from my eyes.

I bore in Greece a burning name,
  And I have been in Italy
Madonna to a painter-lad,
  And mistress to a Medici.

And have you heard (and I have heard)
  Of puzzled men with decorous mien,
Who judged – The wench knows far too much –
  And hanged her on the Salem green?

Wisława Szymborska

BEHEADING

Décolletage comes from decollo,
decollo means I cut off the neck.

The Queen of Scots, Mary Stuart,
approached the scaffold in suitable chemise,
the chemise was décolleté
and red as a burst of blood.

At the very same time
in a deserted chamber
Elizabeth Tudor, Queen of England,
stood by a window in a white dress.
The dress was triumphantly buttoned to the chin
and ended in a starched ruff.

They were thinking in unison:
'Lord, have mercy on me'
'Right is on my side'
'To go on living or else be in the way'
'In certain circumstances the owl is a baker's daughter'
'This will never end'
'This has already ended'
'What am I doing here, where there is nothing.'

A difference in dress – yes, let's be sure of that.
The detail
is immutable.

Translated by A. Maguire and J. Krynski

Gwen Harwood

From SEVEN PHILOSOPHICAL POEMS:
RELIGIOUS INSTRUCTION

My friend and I, put out
from the Old Testament
lesson for giggling, went
and made ourselves from clay
a fine hermaphrodite
idol: huge breasts, the lot.

We sought protection from
teachers and clergymen,
but most, two goatish boys
who took the same road home
calling, 'You've got a womb!
Girls have got wombs!' and worse.

Immediate success!
That self-same day the first
caught smoking was well thrashed,
and the second savaged by
a dog he used to tease.
Versions of this got round.

So we reigned in a blessed
communion of young sinners,
queens of the underworld.
But in secret crumbled God
back to his elements
among riddles never guessed.

Jill Hellyer

JONAH'S WIFE

A likely story, she said.
You fled to Tarshish from
the presence of the Lord
and now you're telling us
you were cast overboard.
A likely story, she said,
climbing cold into her cold bed.

In the belly of a whale!
You, old man, who fear
the Lord's wrath and mine
coming home like this

and spinning such a yarn.
The belly of a whale!
A quaint excuse . . . I know a likelier tale.

A touching story, she said,
to say they cast you out
for being troublesome . . .
and well they might! Your own
wife knows what shores you've swum.
But swallowed by a whale! she said
laughing cold into her cold bed.

Hayashi Fumiko

THE LORD BUDDHA

I fell in love with the Lord Buddha
when I kiss his chill lips sacrilegiously
my heart swoons

from beginning to end
my peaceful blood flows backward
overcome with sacrilegiousness
my heart has been overwhelmed
by the beauty
of his irresistible perfect peace
oh Lord Buddha

Translated by Kenneth Rexroth and I. Atsumi

Ruth Silcock

THE BUDDHA'S WIFE

It can't have been fun for the Buddha's wife,
Left on her own for the rest of her life

When her good lord fled
The royal bed
To seek for his own perfection.

It's said in praise of Mahatma Gandhi –
A sort of saint, though his legs were bandy,
He was skinny and quaint – but still, a saint –
That for years he had nothing to do with his wife:
What about her life?

Christian women wear hats in church,
For fear lest their worshipping husbands lurch
And stagger and stare
At the sight of their hair,
Shining and heavy and long and free;
'Christian women shall not tempt me',
Said stern St Paul, who refused to fall
Twice over, and made all women cover
Their burning and moving hair.

'Come,' said the milkmaids, 'come, come, come',
To their lord, Lord Krishna; who will not come.
The milkmaids dance and cry to the dawn,
White milk, white flowers on an emerald lawn,
The milkmaids call and the tired cows yawn
And nobody comes.

According to men, God has chosen men
To be his voice, his hand, his pen,
To utter his laws, to touch his grace,
To write his books, to read his face,
To be his channel to everyone human
Except a woman.

Pam Thompson

ONCE BITTEN

They weren't talking.
He, sulking
because she wouldn't recognize
the price of apples,
wearily scratched his rib.

It still ached from the fall.

She, heart-sick of gardening,
Brooded over the empty promise
of being clothed.

A crack in the sky
and lightning flashed
through parting clouds.

He gazed, and appreciating once more,
her pale, orginal beauty
tentatively caressed her breast.

'Piss off, Adam,
I've got a headache.'

Máighréad Medbh

ORIGINAL SIN

They tell me my child is a sinner
before he leaves the womb.
Well he must be a wizard
of a Hallowe'en tricker
if he sins while upside down
in a bag of water.

They say we made a sinner
because we made a sin

with the evil diction
of the mutual friction
of the basest parts
of our base bodies.

Now the woman's body is sin
and the baby lying within
is staring down
at the evil crown
of the pagan goddess, Quim?

No, says the Catholic priest,
you're having a pagan feast.
The child is a sinner
because of his flesh.
All human beings
are made of trash.
Every heart that beats
and is not baptised
is in Satan's drum,
synchronised.

So what about God
or is he too big
to jump in the womb
and be infra dig?

DNA is the greatest sin –
Duped with Natural Acumen –
There's my child
with a natural mind
and the churches want to put him
in a moral bind.

But it makes no odds
because my child's a bud
and she'll burst onto earth
like a flower should.
She'll shut up the church
like a jack-in-the-box
and she'll shout 'Up yours'
to the Pope and John Knox.

The Original Witch
will pick up the switch
and turn off the lights
in the steeple's sight.
She will laugh Ha Ha
She will laugh Ho Ho
And the walls will go
just like in Jericho.

Grace Evans

CATECHISM

In my church we pray like this:
with a shimmy and a shake.
Roll, Mama, roll.
Find my bass note and strike it hard.
Give me the mark of exclamation!
God elects the joyous, don't you know?

In my church we pray like this:
with a shimmy and a shake,
a desire to forsake
                    nothing.

Sandra Marshall

THE GIRLS IN THE BIG PICTURE

It was back in the early sixties
When me and my best chum, Pat,
Decided to try something different:
We were scunnered wi' this and wi' that.

Our big night out was a Saturday,
At the Orpheus you'd find us there,

But first to the Viking for a couple of drinks
And a quick check-up on the hair.

We rocked and we rolled and we twisted,
A right pair of ravers back then,
And if we didn't click we wandered on home
With a pastie supper from Ken's.

Then suddenly one day, just outta the blue
I turns round and says to Pat,
'Come on, you and me will join the Air Force.'
Says she til me, 'Why not?'

Our Mas and Das thought us mental
But they didn't object just the same,
so we threw a big going-away party –
I think half of Belfast came.

So off we sailed for England
Not knowing when we'd return.
As we waved goodbye to our families
We both had a good oul gurn.

We arrived next day at lunch-hour,
Both of us knackered and done.
In no time we were out there marchin'.
Stickin' out! The field, here we come.

Well, we couldn't do it for laughin' –
If you'd sen the cut of us –
Till the officer in charge let a gulder,
'Who's causing all that fuss?'

Up at half-past six every morning,
The middle of the night it seemed,
As we stood at our beds like zombies:
For inspection all had to be clean.

The grub we got was rotten,
One luk and we wanted to cry,
'For God's sake wud somebody bring us
A lovely big Ulster fry!'

At a lecture one day they asked us
Who joined just to get a man.
I nearly died, I was cut to the bone
When Pat stuck up her hand.

The officer looked at her odd–like,
She says, 'Is that rightly so?'
Pat just shrugged her shoulders,
'Aye, well, sort of a way, you know.'

Everybody called us Paddy.
That really got on our wick.
By Friday we'd just about had it,
We were starting to feel homesick.

We were sent to the commanding officer
To explain why we wanted out.
Thon oul' doll, I'll never forget her,
She made Hitler luk like a Boy Scout.

'You Irish girls have no backbone,'
She screamed at me and Pat.
'I'm from Belfast and I'd never go back.'
The two of us thought, 'Thank Jesus for that.'

We hadn't tuppence, no boat-fare home.
The Air Force lent us it.
We promised faithfully to pay it back –
They are waitin' on it yit.

We arrived back home on the Saturday,
Not even a full week away.
The sleggins we had to put up with
I've never forgot to this day.

We kept a low profile for ages,
The shame was too much to bear.
I can still hear the fellas shoutin',
'Is that the two rejects there?'

So it was back to the Orpheus on Saturday,
A bit more resigned to things.

To hell with leaving Belfast,
To hell with wanting wings.

Wendy Cope

SISTERS

(for Marian)

My sister
was the bad one –
said what she thought
and did what she liked
and didn't care.

At ten she wore
a knife tucked in
her leather belt,
dreamed of *being*
a prince on a white horse.

Became a dolly bird
with dyed hair longer
than her skirts, pulling
the best of the local talent.
Mother wept and prayed.

At thirty she's divorced,
has cropped her locks
and squats in Hackney –
tells me 'God created man
then realised Her mistake.'

I'm not like her,
I'm good – but now
I'm working on it.
Fighting through
to my own brand of badness

I am glad of her
at last – her conferences,

her anger, and her boots.
We talk and smoke
and laugh at everybody –

two bad sisters.

Jo Crayola

THE REAL ONES

First of all, real ones don't have tattoos,
which counts me out for a start.
They generally shave their armpits
at least the ones you see advertising themselves do;
and they don't sport bruises like these ones,
in these places.
In fact, you could be forgiven for thinking
they didn't even have places like these.

What they do have is laps.
Yes, a lap.
For a cat to sit on, or a baby
or a husband to bury his despairing head.
(And that's another thing I forgot to mention.
They also tend to have husbands.)
For themselves, they never despair.
Or if they do we don't remember it.
Or else we mention it only later
when we grow up and go to therapy.
They are of course warm, soft, enduring,
with their receiving bosoms,
their strong hands,
their sharp tongues
and their worn spirits.
They are excellent for taking on holiday
as they keep up everyone's morale.
Even if it's raining.
Or the campsite's over-booked.

They don't wear nightdresses like this one.
They don't wipe snotty little faces
with a corner of their t-shirt.
Or wear monkey boots, refuse to comb their hair,
or allow a
very small boy
to wash their back in the bath.

No! They are entirely different. Look at them,
chatting together in the doctors' waiting room,
prowling the shops, pushing buggies, yanking toddlers.
Some of them are younger than me, blonder, skinnier,
yet still seem to manage it.
They are the *real ones*,
watching at hospital bedsides, soothing foreheads, plastering
knees, buttoning coats and remembering wellies;
serving up tissues, fruit and aspirins
at every impromptu picnic.

One day I suppose I'll join them,
when I've had the tattoo erased by laser,
given up scoffing the sweets he brings home from parties,
grown a lap, and a husband and a hairless armpit;
stopped lying on my bed listening to loud music
when I should be making the tea.

I don't know how exactly it happens,
but I'm waiting for it
(and meanwhile watching *Neighbours*, to get in practice)

I only hope that when it does,
he will have the grace
to be a teeny-weeny bit,
ever-so-slightly

disappointed.

Hattie Gossett

DREADLOCK OFFICE TEMP/LABOR RELATIONS NO.5

she has long dreadlocks & she wears loud colors & big earrings &
either red or orange goldflecked nail polish on her finger&toe nails.
in summer she wears hiheeled open shoes with no stockings on
her big fine hairy legs. neither does she shave under her arms. she
is too trifling to wear makeup every day. she sits in an unventilated
little backroom of a wall street corporate tower & types 100words
per minute on the word processor. in the elevator & ladies room
& cafeteria the grey flannel people with their blow drys & perms
& jerry curls stare at her. they ask her how she got her hair like
that. she tells them she stopped combing it. when they recoil aghast
she encourages them to try it too. just stop combing your hair she
tells them.

Anon, 1938

'SHE WAS POOR BUT SHE WAS HONEST'

She was poor but she was honest,
    Victim of a rich man's game;
First he loved her, then he left her,
    And she lost her maiden name.

Then she hastened up to London,
    For to hide her grief and shame;
There she met another rich man,
    And she lost her name again.

See her riding in her carriage,
    In the Park and all so gay;
All the nibs and nobby persons
    Come to pass the time of day.

See them in the gay theater
    Sitting in the costly stalls;
With one hand she holds the programme,
    With the other she strokes his hand.

See him have her dance in Paris
  In her frilly underclothes;
All those Frenchies there applauding
  When she strikes a striking pose.

See the little country village
  Where her aged parents live;
Though they drink champagne she sends them,
  Still they never can forgive.

In the rich man's arms she flutters
  Like a bird with a broken wing;
First he loved her, then he left her,
  And she hasn't got a ring.

See him in his splendid mansion
  Entertaining with the best,
While the girl he has ruined
  Entertains a sordid guest.

See him riding in his carriage
  Past the gutter where she stands;
He has made a stylish marriage
  While she wrings her ringless hands.

See him in the House of Commons
  Passing laws to put down crime,
While the victim of his passions
  Slinks away to hide her shame.

See her on the bridge at midnight
  Crying 'Farewell, faithless love!'
There's a scream, a splash – Good Heavens!
  What is she a-doing of?

Then they dragged her from the river,
  Water from her clothes they wrung;
They all thought that she was drownded,
  But the corpse got up and sung:

'It's the same the whole world over;
  It's the poor as gets the blame,
It's the rich as gets the pleasure –
  Aint it all a bleeding shame!'

Ann Ziety

'I DON'T LOOK LIKE KIM BASINGER'

I don't look like Kim Basinger
No tits, no arse, no pout, no curves
No Vidal Sassoon hairdo
No Christian Dior casuals
In fact I'm hardly female –
Look more like a gerbil.

But can't say I'm too annoyed
Cos at least I don't have to get screwed
By Batman or Dan Ackroyd.

Maggie Christie

THE TOOTH FAIRY

I am
The Tooth Fairy
 Doubling as Santa Claws.
Just lose a tooth
 Lose a tooth? How careless can you get?
And I'll be there
Any day of the year
 Days?
 Since when did I get to work days?
I work while you sleep
But I never sleep
I fly over the world
To watch children lose teeth.
 Stupid thing to reward.
Overtime? What's that?
 Double nothing is nothing.
Join a union? Why?
 They wouldn't take me.
But sometimes – I'm sorry –

I forget the way
        Get drunk
Or didn't notice a toothipeg
Till the next day
        Someone didn't tell their mum?
        Why apologise anyway?

I am the Tooth and Claws Fairy
I travel round subverting little girls
persuading them their best friends are each other
and Christmas is a lie about a father
(or else that Mary was a surrogate mother)
and losing teeth is just a bloody nuisance . . .
and speaking of a bloody nuisance –
you know what I mean, the real bloody nuisance –
why isn't that provided with a fairy?

Win Baker

WAITING

The couple
married a long time
live in uneasy truce
waiting

neither cares
for the way the house looks

if he were gone
she'd sell his tools
burn bits of lumber

if she goes first
he'll throw out
books and pictures

won't ask
the family if they want them

solicitously inquire
How do you feel today?

Nilene O.A. Foxworth

SHO NUFF

Cold soft drinks
quenched my thirst
one hot and humid July day
after a cool drive
to a mountain store.
Seems like every woman
in the place
had on halter tops
displaying their expensive tans.
There were two women
standing in front of me
at the checkout counter.
One said to the other,
'You must be a lady of leisure,
just look at your beautiful tan.'
Then the other woman responded,
'No, you must be a lady of leisure,
yours is much darker than mine.'
A tall dark and handsome Black dude
standing behind me
whispering down my Black back
s

  a

   i

   d
'Sister, if those two
are ladies of leisure,
you must surely be
a lady of royalty.'
And in a modest tone, I replied,
'SHO NUFF?'

Fiona Pitt-Kethley

SKY RAY LOLLY

A toddler on a day out in Herne Bay,
on seeing an ancient, civil-servant-type,
I held my Sky Ray lolly – red, yellow
and green striped, pointed, dripping down between
my legs and walked bandy. My Ma and Pa,
(old-fashioned innocents like Rupert Bear's),
just didn't notice this and ambled on,
that is, until they saw the old man's face,
jaw dislocated in surprise. They grabbed
that Martian's willy from my little hand.

The world still sees me as a nasty kid
usurping maleness. A foul brat to be
smacked down by figures of authority.
All things most natural in men, in me
are vice – having no urge to cook or clean,
lacking maternal instincts.

And they would take my pride, my rocket
of ambition, amputate my fun and geld
my laughter, depriving me of colour.
And smirk to see my little lolly melt,
me left with a stick.

Gladys Mary Coles

THE POSEDOWN

Without my glasses I can't see the audience or judges
but I hear the reaction as I flex my oiled bunches
solid as Spanish onions, shiny as conkers.
In the glass Superdrome I'm hoping to make the posedown,
to figure prominently in the Middleweight division.
My striations are sure to please. Today my definition's
clearer than ever before, torso muscles honed –
in sharp detail. The last six weeks self-sculpting,

ripping off (see my ribbed veins), regime of iron,
liver liquid, anabolic packs, has certainly paid off
moulding my Michelangelo manshape.

I'm pumping up now. Five strung-out minutes until
they call the top six. I just know I'll be selected,
onstage again, performing (as Schwarzenneger says) my art.
This thigh pose should stop the show, and here's
my ultimate creative position. It's a pity though
that Sonia dislikes my skin – 'like overdone sirloin'.
Nasty, that. No excuse, even if she is vegetarian
and breeds prize Siamese. Jealous as well, maybe,
knowing how Julie admires my deltoid routine, oils
my double biceps. But Sonia gives me no back-up
not even nutritional, neglecting my collagen, my adrenal
hormones. Julie though, after workout, is always there
feeding me dessert spoons of raw amino elixir.
This won't do. I must concentrate on myself, project
my mental prime. I've peaked on time. Confidence
is all I need to win. If I do, Julie's promised me
that blue dumbell kit. The names are being called . . .
'Jane Phipps'. Yippee!

Alice Moore

THREE MEN

There ain't but three men
                    who really can spend my dough
There ain't but three men
                    who really can spend my dough
There's the rent man, the grocery man
                                and the man that owns the
                                clothing store

There's only three men
                    that can flag this train of mine
There's only three men
                    that can flag this train of mine

There's the working man and the gambler
>   and the one that loves me
>   all the time

There ain't but three men
>   that I really won't treat wrong
There ain't but three men
>   that I really won't treat wrong
That's my father and my brother
>   and the one that lays on my arm

There ain't but three men
>   who can make a clown out of me
There ain't but three men
>   who can make a clown out of me
That's my husband and my sweetheart
>   and my old-time used-to-be

There ain't but three men
>   who really can make me fall
There ain't but three men
>   who really can make me fall
That's my *best* friend, my kid man,
>   the one that's kicking in my stall

Berta R. Freistadt

A LETTER ABOUT MILESTONES

Dear Marg
When we are fifty
We will be very old
And if not
We will try harder
And look down
Our noses
At noisy young things
And pretend
To have headaches

And important wisdoms
To discuss
We will polish
Our white hair
On the stones
Of our experience
And keep quiet
About many things
Most of it
in fact.
For they must do
Their suffering
In their time
And wont be told
Anymore
Than we were

When we are fifty
Dear
We will look
Marvellous and
They'll all say you
Dont look
Fifty
And we can look
Quite rightly cross
And snap
Of course we do

At fifty dear
We wont have to
Wear polo-neck
Sweaters to hide
Our scraggy necks
We can have
Plunging neck lines
To remind ourselves
And let them
Worry about
How it looks

At fifty dear
We may have learnt
Nothing
But only we
Will know

Maria Banuş

THE LOST CHILD

Panic in my dream:
God, I can't be forty,
I'm still a child.
How have I failed you?

I wake up.
Light filters through the blinds.
It's morning. I'm seventy.
Humble ecstasy of being.

Translated by Andrea Deletant
and Brenda Walker

Sappho

'I HEAR THAT ANDROMEDA –'

I hear that Andromeda –

That hayseed in her hay-
seed finery – has put
a torch to your heart

and she without even
the art of lifting her
skirt over her ankles

Translated by Mary Barnard

'If they can't take a joke . . .'

Sylvia Kantaris

BLUFF

It takes a certain savoir-faire to give a paper on
some area of deconstructionism when
I don't know what it means and can't even read yet.
Naturally I'm also entirely naked.

Still, I stun the auditorium of learned
scholars in the field of studies pioneered
by someone foreign with my startling contribution:
'We need to strip bananas down to basics, Gentlemen.'

And then I swing down from the rostrum without bothering
to register the thunderous ovation, having
no time whatsoever to appear at my next lecture
on post–deconstructionism in Geneva.

I am correctly dressed, in grey, when I arrive
to find the auditorium already packed with
pitifully naked deconstructionists
still stripping bananas in many languages.

Anon, Morocco

AN ANCIENT SONG OF A WOMAN OF FEZ

I see a man who is dull
and boring like no one else.

He is heavier than massive mountains.
When he laughs he shakes the plains of Gharb,
when he cries the coastal cities tremble.

To look at an ugly man
gives me a headache.

Translated by Willis Barnstone

Gillian Allnutt

THATCHERTHICKY

'Twas April, and the poxly caws
Did gawg and garble in the Hooze:
All stortsy were the leftygigs,
And the rightly nobs in booze.

'Beware the Thatcherthick, my son!
The eyes that stare, the pearls that catch!
Beware the Bakerbod, and shun
The budgetous Majorsnatch!'

He took his rebate application form in hand:
Long time the Polltax foe he sought –
So rested he by tall Big Ben,
And stood awhile in thought.

And as in plotly thought he stood,
The Thatcherthick, with eyes of gold,
Came direct-debiting through his thoughts,
And grubbled as it strolled!

One, two! One, two! And up and down
The rebate form went slipper-slap!
He left it dead, and with its head (or poll)
He went tackswiggling back.

'And hast thou slain the Thatcherthick?
Come to my arms, my unratable boy!
O hopslick day! We need not pay!'
He chortled in his joy.

'Twas April, and the poxly caws
Did gawg and garble in the Hooze:
All stortsy were the leftygigs,
And the rightly nobs in booze.

Alison Chisholm

OFFICE PARTY

I think I enjoyed the party.
I cannot remember it well.
My stomach is churning in circles
and my poor head is hurting like hell.

I think I enjoyed the buffet,
but the crab paste was long past its best.
The quiche was awash with heaven knows what
and the salad was limp and depressed.

The cheese cubes on sticks were all crusted,
the vol-au-vents soggy and stale,
the trifle was dusted with fag ash
and smelt less of sherry than ale.

I think I enjoyed the fruit cup,
and a glass of the manager's wine.
The gin and the Scotch and the vodka
all left me feeling just fine.

The problems began with the brandy –
one sip of it went to my head.
I remember removing my stockings,
and then . . . oh, I wish I was dead.

I seem to remember the records,
they played all my favourite sounds.
I started the conga to 'Nights in White Satin'
and cha-cha'd to 'Send in the Clowns.'

Then somebody danced on the table
and sat on the manager's knee,
and did something crude with the manager's hat,
and – oh glory, I think it was me.

My memory's starting to focus.
I remember the manager's face
when I told him I hated the work and the staff
and just what he could do with the place.

I think I enjoyed the party –
one over the eight is no crime,
but reviewing last night in the cold light of day,
I think I had better resign.

Annie Blue

IF THE CAP FITS

To the tune of Jingle Bells . . .

CHORUS   Jingle pills
dangle coils,
condoms three a day,
oh what fun
it is to risk
your life for
him this way.

Dashing from the clinic
with a bagful of supplies,
orthogel, nonoxyl nine
and a new cap tried for size.
Basking in the glow
of responsibility,
oh what fun it is to know
you control your destiny.

CHORUS   Oh Jingle pills . . . etc.

The 'Dalkon Shield' is out,
there's a compensation boom,
it caused infection and its
barbs got embedded in your womb.
Sponges made such mess,
they never did catch on
but there's a condom now for girls
so all his worry's gone.

CHORUS   Oh Jingle pills . . . etc.

'Just a question, dear!'
the nurse shouts from the loo,
'Have you had your smear?'
The whole queue stares at you.
'Ah yes I have it here,
your notes say you're okay,
just inflammation, don't fret dear.
Will the next one come this way.'

CHORUS   Oh Jingle pills . . . etc.

Dashing to the clinic
to be first in STD,
don't panic if it's gone too far
hysterectomies are free.
Legs up in the air,
do the gyne dance,
these are the steps of heterosex,
skipped over in romance.

CHORUS   Oh Jingle pills . . . etc.

No one mentioned AIDS,
VD or NSU,
trichonomas was, you thought,
something magicians do.
Cancer can be screened
and really you're not ill
with 'side effects' like heart disease
from ten years on the pill.

CHORUS   Oh Jingle pills . . . etc.

Amryl Johnson

GRANNY IN DE MARKET PLACE

Yuh fish fresh?

Woman, why yuh holdin' meh fish up tuh yuh nose?
De fish fresh. Ah say it fresh. Ah ehn go say it any mo'

Hmmm, well if dis fish fresh den is I who dead an' gone
De ting smell like it take a bath in a lavatory in town
It here so long it happy. Look how de mout' laughin' at we
De eye turn up to heaven like it want tuh know 'e fate
Dey say it does take a good week before dey reach dat state

Yuh mango ripe?

Gran'ma, stop feelin' and squeezin' up meh fruit!
Yuh ehn playin' in no ban'. Meh mango eh no concertina

Ah tell yuh dis mango hard just like yuh face
One bite an' ah sure tuh break both ah meh plate
If yuh cahn tell de difference between green an' rosy red
dohn clim' jus' wait until dey fall down from de tree
Yuh go know dey ripe when de lizard an dem start tuh feed
but dohn bring yuh force-ripe fruit tuh try an' sell here
it ehn burglars is crooks like yuh poor people have to fear

De yam good?

Old lady, get yuh nails outta meh yam!
Ah mad tuh make yuh buy it now yuh damage it so bad

Dis yam look like de one dat did come off ah de ark
She brother in de Botanical Gardens up dey by Queens Park
Tourists with dey camera comin' from all over de worl'
takin' pictures dey never hear any yam could be dat ole
Ah have a crutch an' a rocking-chair someone give meh fuh free
If ah did now ah would ah bring dem an' leave dem here fuh she

De bush clean?

Well, I never hear more! Old woman, is watch yuh watching meh
young young dasheen leaf wit' de dew still shinin' on dem!

It seem tuh me like dey does like tuh lie out in de sun
jus' tuh make sure dat dey get dey edges nice an' brown
an' maybe is weight dey liftin' tuh made dem look so tough
Dey wan' build up dey strength fuh when tings start gettin'
rough
Is callaloo ah makin' but ah 'fraid things get too hot
Yuh bush go want tuh fight an' meh crab go jump outta de pot

How much a poun' yuh fig?

Ah have a big sign tellin' yuh how much it cos'
Yuh either blin' yuh dotish or yuh jus' cahn read at all

Well, ah wearin' meh glasses so ah readin' yuh big big sign
but tuh tell yuh de trut' ah jus' cahn believe meh eye
Ah lookin' ah seein' but no man could be so blasted bol'
Yuh mus' tink dis is Fort Knox yuh sellin' fig as if is gol'
Dey should put all ah all yuh somewhere nice an' safe
If dey close Sing-Song prison dat go be the bestest place

De orange sweet?

Ma, it eh hah orange in dis market as sweet as ah does sell
It like de sun, it taste like sugar an' it juicy as well

Yuh know, boy, what yuh sayin' have a sorta ring
De las' time ah buy yuh tell meh exactly de same ting
When ah suck ah fin' all dem sour as hell
De dentures drop out an' meh two gums start tuh swell
Meh mout' so sore ah cahn even eat ah meal
Yuh sure it ehn lime all yuh wrappin' in orange peel?

De coconut hah water?

Chrystos

POEM FOR LETTUCE

I know
you don't want to be eaten

anymore than a cow or a pig or a chicken does
but   they're the vicious vegetarians
& they say you do
Gobbling up the innocent green beings who gladden
any reasonable person's heart
   I'll tell you little lettuce
you'll see them in cowskin shoes & belts
   & nobody can make sense of that
Those virtuous vegetarians they'll look at you with prim distaste
   while you enjoy your bacon
            Makes me want
to buy some cowboy movie blood capsules
   Imagine an introduction
I'd like you to meet Lily, she's a non-smoking non-drinking
vegetarian separatist Pisces with choco-phobia
& I smile
while secretly biting down on the capsules concealed in my cheeks
   then shake her hand   drooling blood
I whisper
Hi   I'm a flaming carnivorous double Scorpio who'll eat anything
& as she wilts in dismay   trembles with trepidation
hisses with disgust
Ah   then   little lettuces
   we'll have our moment of laughing revenge

   For Elizabeth Markell

Liz Lochhead

FAVOURITE SHADE

   (Rap)

   She's getting No More Black, her.
   You've got bugger all bar black, Barbra.
   Black's dead drab an' all.
   Ah'd never have been seen
   deid in it, your age tae!

Dreich. As a shade it's draining.
Better aff
somethin tae pit a bit a colour in her cheeks,
   eh no?

Aphra Behn

THE DISAPPOINTMENT

I.

One day the Amorous *Lysander*,
By an impatient Passion sway'd,
Surpriz'd fair *Cloris*, that lov'd Maid,
Who could defend her self no longer.
All things did with his Love conspire;
The gilded Planet of the Day,
In his gay Chariot drawn by Fire,
Was now descending to the Sea,
And left no Light to guide the World,
But what from *Cloris* Brighter Eyes was hurld.

II.

In a lone Thicket made for Love,
Silent as yielding Maids Consent,
She with a Charming Languishment,
Permits his Force, yet gently strove;
Her Hands his Bosom softly meet,
But not to put him back design'd,
Rather to draw 'em on inclin'd:
Whilst he lay trembling at her Feet,
Resistance 'tis in vain to show;
She wants the pow'r to say – *Ah! What d'ye do?*

III.

Her Bright Eyes sweet, and yet severe,
Where Love and Shame confus'dly strive,

Fresh Vigor to *Lysander* give;
And breathing faintly in his Ear,
She cry'd – *Cease, Cease – your vain Desire,*
Or I'll call out – What would you do?
My Dearer Honour ev'n to You
I cannot, must not give – Retire,
Or take this Life, whose chiefest part
I gave you with the Conquest of my Heart.

IV.

But he as much unus'd to Fear,
As he was capable of Love,
The blessed minutes to improve,
Kisses her Mouth, her Neck, her Hair;
Each Touch her new Desire Alarms.
His burning trembling Hand he prest
Upon her swelling Snowy Brest,
While she lay panting in his Arms.
All her Unguarded Beauties lie
The Spoils and Trophies of the Energy.

V.

And now without Respect or Fear,
He seeks the Object of his Vows,
(His Love no Modesty allows)
By swift degrees advancing – where
His daring Hand that Altar seiz'd,
Where Gods of Love do sacrifice:
That Awful Throne, that Paradice
Where Rage is calm'd, and Anger pleas'd;
That Fountain where Delight still flows,
And gives the Universal World Repose.

VI.

Her balmy lips countring his,
as their Souls, are joyn'd;
both in Transports Unconfin'd
extend themselves upon the Moss.
Cloris half dead and breathless lay;
Her soft Eyes cast a Humid Light,

Such as divides the Day and Night;
Or falling Stars, whose Fires decay:
And now no signs of Life she shows,
But what in short breath'd Sighs returns and goes.

   VII.

He saw how at her length she lay;
He saw her rising Bosom bare;
Her loose thin *Robes*, through which appear
A Shape design'd for Love and Play;
Abandon'd by her Pride and Shame.
She does her softest Joys dispence,
Off'ring her Virgin-Innocence
A Victim to Loves Sacred Flame;
While the o'er-Ravish'd Shepherd lies
Unable to perform the Sacrifice.

   VIII.

Ready to taste a thousand Joys,
The too transported hapless Swain
Found the vast Pleasure turn'd to Pain;
Pleasure which too much Love destroys:
The willing Garments by he laid,
And Heaven all open'd to his view,
Mad to possess, himself he threw
On the Defenceless Lovely Maid.
But Oh what envying God conspires
To snatch his Power, yet leave him the Desire.

   IX.

Nature's Support, (without whose Aid
She can no Humane Being give)
It self now wants the Art to live;
Faintness its slack'ned Nerves invade:
In vain th'inraged Youth essay'd
To call its fleeting Vigor back,
No motion 'twill from Motion take;
Excess of Love is Love betray'd:
In vain he Toils, in vain Commands,
Then I sensible fell weeping in his Hand.

X.

In this so Amorous Cruel Strife,
Where Love and Fate were too severe
The poor *Lysander* in despair
Renounc'd his Reason with his Life
Now all the brisk and active Fire
That should the Nobler Part inflame,
Serv'd to increase his Rage and Shame
And left no Spark for New Desire:
Not all her Naked Charms cou'd move
Or calm that Rage that had debauch'd his Love.

XI.

Cloris returning from the Trance
Which Love and soft Desire had bred,
Her timerous Hand she gently laid
(Or guided by Design or Chance)
Soon that Fabulous *Priapus*,
That Potent God, as Poets feign;
But never did young *Shepherdess*,
Gath'ring of Fern upon the Plain,
nimbly draw her Fingers back,
Finding beneath the verdant Leaves a Snake.

U. A. Fanthorpe

NOT MY BEST SIDE

[I]

Not my best side, I'm afraid.
The artist didn't give me a chance to
Pose properly, and as you can see,
Poor chap, he had this obsession with
Triangles, so he left off two of my
Feet. I didn't comment at the time
(What, after all, are two feet

To a monster?) but afterwards
I was sorry for the bad publicity.
Why, I said to myself, should my conqueror
Be so ostentatiously beardless, and ride
A horse with a deformed neck and square hoofs?
Why should my victim be so
Unattractive as to be inedible, .
And why should she have me literally
On a string? I don't mind dying
Ritually, since I always rise again,
But I should have liked a little more blood
To show they were taking me seriously.

[II]

It's hard for a girl to be sure if
She wants to be rescued. I mean, I quite
Took to the dragon. It's nice to be
Liked, if you know what I mean. He was
So nicely physical, with his claws
And lovely green skin, and that sexy tail,
And the way he looked at me.

He made me feel he was all ready to
Eat me. And any girl enjoys that.
So when this boy turned up, wearing machinery,
On a really *dangerous* horse, to be honest,
I didn't much fancy him. I mean,
What was he like underneath the hardware?
He might have acne, blackheads or even
Bad breath for all I could tell, but the dragon –
Well, you could see all his equipment
At a glance. Still, what could I do?
The dragon got himself beaten by the boy,
And a girl's got to think of her future.

[III]

I have diplomas in Dragon
Management and Virgin Reclamation.
My horse is the latest model, with

Automatic transmission and built-in
Obsolescence. My spear is custom-built,
And my prototype armour
Still on the secret list. You can't
Do better than me at the moment.
I'm qualified and equipped to the
Eyebrow. So why be difficult?
Don't you want to be killed and/or rescued
In the most contemporary way? Don't
You want to carry out the roles
That sociology and myth have designed for you?
Don't you realize that, by being choosy,
You are endangering job prospects
In the spear- and horse-building industries?
What, in any case, does it matter what
You want? You're in my way.

Vicki Raymond

ON SEEING THE FIRST FLASHER

Grey-coated, solitary stranger, hail!
Thou harbinger of summer's lusty days,
tracing through country parks thy mazy trail,
or lingering by some brook to catch the gaze
of passing schoolgirl, who, with scornful eye,
remarks upon thy manhood's lack of length,
then vanishing, before her angry cry
shall summon to her aid the studded strength
of forty skinheads, or, with deadly aim,
her dainty foot shall plunge into thy crotch—
when shalt thou find a partner to thy game,
a maid whose pleasure is to stand and watch?
As soon, alas, as poets shall enthrall
commuter crowds, or fill the Albert Hall.

Maria Jastrzębska

WHICH OF US WEARS THE TROUSERS

Behind the liberal politeness
You're dying to know
Instead of the chat about societal attitudes
What you'd really like to ask is
Which of us in this relationship
Wears the trousers.

I'll tell you
Since you want to know so much
And since it's really very simple:
I do
And then again
She does
And then sometimes
Neither of us
Wears any trousers at all.

Anna Swir

GO TO THE CINEMA

I'm equally happy
whether you're arriving or leaving.
So you give me
two kinds of happiness.

But don't come round today.
I have guests. They're called
Bored with Romantic Ritual,
Eternity's Sneer, and
Disgust.

They're foreigners. You don't know their language.
Better go to the cinema
and see a western.

Translated by Grazyna Baran and
Margaret Marshment

Anon, Chinese folk

'HOW CAN HOME GROWN SCALLIONS'

How can home grown scallions
smell as fragrant as wild ones?
My husband's words fall like hard sticks.
My lover mouths words of wild honey.

Translated by Cecilia Liang

Ann Dancy

'YOU'LL BE FINE'

Take aspirin. Take plenty.'
But you sigh, readjust your elbow,
rest your face on the teapot.
'Yes. Heat. That really works.
Sometimes.' There's no rush.
You have a whole morning
to nurse the headache, to decide.

When Alice arrives, you kiss her
and go out to patrol the garden;
your jeans ripped in the wrong place,
your baggy political t-shirt,
your familiar profile oddly cut
and recut by the sheets, the nappies.
I share the beer with her.

Three years, two kids and it's on.
A few friends told. No family. No flowers.
'You O.K.?' she shouts.
Thumbs up from you, who are, after all,
alright. Even sober. Even today.
And I notice you've recovered the shears
from the hedge and are about to tangle

with the clematis or Russian Vine
or whatever it is . . . 'What *is* that?'

'That's him', she says, 'Whittling over nothing.
Hardly a major operation, is it? Vasectomy.'
You look back. We raise our cans to you.

M. S. Lumsden

NAE ME

I doot ye maun say that again.
  I've tint ma thummle.
Growin deef?   Nae me!   I can hear ye fine
  fin ye dinna mummle.

Thank ye!   I'll threed my needle masel,
  Na, I'm nae growin blin.
Nae me!   It's this licht and this ee's ower sma
  to lat the threed in.

Aye, I'm comin.   It's nae me that's slow.   Ye're ower fest
  that's the truth o' the maiter.
Twisna the hare won the race, ye maun min;
  the aul tortoise did better.

Fiona Pitt-Kethley

A PIECE OF JADE

The first class in a course on Chinese Art –
we sat around, fulsomely holding forth
on tiny objects that our tutor'd brought,
all small enough to be hand held by us,
useful things, he'd said, everyday objects,
some obvious, some not, all well-crafted,
carved and polished to great smoothness.
One struck us by its simple elegance;

our Philippino lecturer looked on,
amused by our pretentiousness. (Although,
we later heard the tale of how he'd won
a grant to set up an illicit still
and urinated at a festival,
distilled it, drunk it and then peed again –
a symbol of the earth's renewal, of course –
and, if you're not too squeamish, a nice way
to earn your bread.) He soon let out, the long
and subtly-polished piece of jade I held
was an old arsehole-stopper from a corpse,
set there to keep the evil spirits out.

Jan Sellers

YOUNG LOVE: A HEALTH & SAFETY POEM

Please don't make love in the showers, dears,
the staff don't like it at all;
it's not that they think that it's rude, dears:
they're afraid that you'll slip and you'll fall.
It's not that we're prejudiced, honest –
we've talked all this over for hours –
but the Centre just isn't insured, dears,
for dykes making love in the showers!

We know that it's fun in the showers, dears
(we wish we had thought of it too)
but we fear we'll be sued for our lives, dears,
should anything happen to you!
Just think of your friends and your families,
this could cause no end of distress;
and if you break your neck in the showers, dears,
then what can we say to the press?

We know that you like to be clean, dears,
that's why you make love in the showers;
but why not go out to the park, dears,

the sprinklers are left on for hours;
why not go home for a bath, dears,
and do it in bubbles instead?
Or be like the rest of us here, dears,
and go home and make love in bed.

I hear that the Governing Body
have said that this practice must stop.
It's an issue they hadn't expected,
it's caught the poor dears on the hop . . .
but they have got an excellent solution,
that – well, nearly everyone likes:
it's 'one at a time' in the showers from now on –
but they've built a jacuzzi for dykes!

Izumi Shikibu

'I USED TO SAY'
Returning home near dawn after a night away

I used to say,
'How poetic,'
but now I know
this dawn-rising men do
is merely tiresome!

Translated by Jane Hirshfield
with Mariko Aratani

Liz Lochhead

EVERYBODY'S MOTHER

Of course
everybody's mother always and
so on . . .

Always never
loved you enough
or too smothering much.

Of course you were the Only One, your
mother
a machine
that shat out siblings, listen

everybody's mother
was the original Frigid-
aire Icequeen clunking out
the hardstuff in nuggets, mirror
silvers and ice-splinters that'd stick
in your heart.

Absolutely everyone's mother
was artistic when she was young.

Everyone's mother
was a perfumed presence with pearls, remote
white shoulders when she
bent over in her ball dress
to kiss you in your crib.

Everybody's mother slept with the butcher
for sausages to stuff you with.

Everyone's mother
mythologised herself. You got mixed up
between dragon's teeth and blackmarket stockings.

Naturally
she failed to give you
Positive Feelings
about your own sorry
sprouting body (it was a bloody shame)

but she did
sit up all night sewing sequins
on your carnival costume

so you would have a good time

and she spat
on the corner of her hanky and scraped
at your mouth with sour lace till you squirmed
so you would look smart

And where
was your father all this time?
Away
at the war, or
in his office, or any-
way conspicuous for his
Absence, so

what if your mother did
float around above you
big as a barrage balloon
blocking out the light?

Nobody's mother can't not never do nothing right.

Adjoah Andoh

C'MON JESSE

ha! she's asleep!
the cry that crosses days and nights.
ha! she's asleep!
hurtle downstairs to the bathroom for a shit – push!
time for a bath?
nah, better not risk it – settle for a wash eh.
ha! she's asleep!
start those letters, fill in the accounts,
do some writing, pay those bills.
ha! she's asleep!
i don't mind if she wakes up, she can cry on the tube,
of course i'll breastfeed her!
well, what do you want me to do – let my daughter
    starve to death?!

ha! she's asleep!
ah leave it! put your feet up!
time for a cig, a beer, dynasty!
ha! she's asleep!
please don't wake up again,
if i don't get some sleep soon i'll die . . .
oh? she's asleep.
c'mon jesse, wake up! – i want to play now!
honestly! some babies are SO boring . . .

Anon

DIAMOND LILY

Oh, my name is Diamond Lily,
I'm a whore in Piccadilly,
And my father runs a brothel in the Strand.
My brother sells his arsehole
To the Guards at Windsor Castle,
We're the finest fucking family in the land.

Dorothy Parker

RESUMÉ

Razors pain you;
Rivers are damp;
Acids stain you;
And drugs cause cramp.
Guns aren't lawful;
Nooses give;
Gas smells awful;
You might as well live.

Jill Dawson

PÆAN

to my child
with his tiny
pod of a penis

O, how I love to
smother it in kisses,
douse it with vanilla talc:
that butter-pale catkin
of downy-soft skin.

His clear yellow urine
– I'm not taking the piss –
only meaning to praise:
       smallness
       friendliness.

O, at last, to *love*
not to envy it
– which has deflowered no one,
penetrated nothing, caused
no more offence than
a chipolata sausage.   Uncooked.

To think,
all were button mushrooms once,
every last one
sweet and temperate.
Such monuments I would make to it!
The Buds of Stonehenge,
Cleopatra's Thimble,
the Eiffel Thumb.

O, but how my son
will curse me, at twenty
reading this.
So proud will he be
of his grown-up
       penis.

Wendy Cope

VERSE FOR A BIRTHDAY CARD

Many happy returns and good luck
When it comes to a present, I'm stuck.
 If you weren't far away
 On your own special day,
I could give you a really nice glass of lager.

Alison Chisholm

LIMERICK

A sadistic young woman from Spain
said she found oral sex a real pain.
 She bit off the tools
 of a dozen poor fools
who tried to convert her in vain.

Jane Barnes

ROUTINE CHECKUP

love said at the dentist's   there for her checkup
she was reading the new Redbook   a survey on your
sexual IQ for couples   so she took the quiz to see how
we're doing   now three years in a bedroom a combination
of wonder and comfy routine   a big dose of TV   and
books scattered on each side of the bed   she said

we did great on compatible levels of frequency
ability to ask for a nubbing of the mizzle and all those
other now very popular things in fact we received a

perfect A minus she said   I wanted to know
what did we get the minus for   she said it wasn't
too bad   just our nighties tended to be ripped up
T shirts and were supposed to be

sexy and attractive and I guess starched by maids
and what we both tended toward was men's extra
large Fruit of the Loom ragged and well loved but   frankly
not pretty so we agreed to go shopping together one of
these days   study up   so when next we take the quiz
we'll know what   sheep's clothing is

Stevie Smith

ADVICE TO YOUNG CHILDREN

'Children who paddle where the ocean bed shelves steeply
Must take great care they do not,
Paddle too deeply.'

Thus spake the awful aging couple
Whose heart the years had turned to rubble.

But the little children, to save any bother,
Let it in at one ear and out at the other.

Jennifer Maiden

NOSE

Dogs have vulnerable big noses.
Cats have dry retentive ones.
She has many books of animals.
At first she enthused over dogs
but now cats too are a pleasure.
She will say 'elephant', but its nose
is the thing that she really touches.
My own nose is quite grandiose:
surprising and secure –
a good thing she can grip
and say with enjoyable
vowel elongation:
'Nose.' In some societies
the nose is a sexual organ, with
its tendency to grow cold and its
propensity to bleed. The bone
in it when pressed feels deeply
good or bad but its skin
is smooth and lacks sensation.
The idea of the nose as erotic
makes violence seem more poignant
perhaps less possible. I fear
her awareness of noses will be
made too abstract by time. I hope
my nose when it's cartooned by age
touches wellbeing in her . . .

Anon, Chinese folk

'I SIP GRUEL'

I sip gruel,
drink soup.
I look at my husband.
My lover is January plum blossoms,
almond flowers in February,
peach petals in March.
My husband yellows,
a soggy April cabbage.

Translated by Cecilia Liang

Jackie Kay

THE VISIT

I thought I'd hid everything
that there wasnie wan
give away sign Left

I put Marx Engels Lenin (no Trotsky)
in the airing cupboard – she'll no be
checking out the towels surely

All the copies of the *Daily Worker*
I shoved under the sofa
the dove of peace I took down from the loo

A poster of Paul Robeson
saying give him his passport
I took down from the kitchen

I left a bust of Burns
my detective stories
and the *Complete Works of Shelley*

She comes at 11.30 exactly.
I pour her coffee
from my new Hungarian set

And foolishly prays she willnae
ask its origins – honestly
this baby is going to my head

She crosses her legs on the sofa
I fancy I hear the *Daily Workers*
rustle underneath her

Well she says, you have an interesting home
She sees my eyebrows rise
It's different she qualifies

Hell and I've spent all morning
trying to look ordinary
– a lovely home for the baby

She buttons her coat all smiles
I'm thinking
I'm on the home run

But just as we get to the last post
her eye catches at the same time as mine
a red ribbon with twenty world peace badges

Clear as a hammer and sickle
on the wall
oh she says are you against nuclear weapons?

To Hell with this. Baby or no baby.
Yes   I says. Yes yes yes.
I'd like this baby to live in a nuclear free environment

Oh. Her eyes light up.
I'm all for peace myself she says
and sits down for another cup of coffee.

Elizabeth Frances Amherst

THE WELFORD WEDDING

Susan and Charlotte and Letty and all
Jump and skip and caper and brawl,
   Frisk in the drawing-room, romp in the hall,
Susan and Charlotte and Letty and all.
   Hark! the fiddle each gay spirit moves;
See, the beaux have all drawn on their gloves.
      Mr Archer will dance,
      And Jack Hobland will prance,
      And Jack Shirley'll advance,
      If my Lady approves.
Chorus: Susan and Charlotte and Letty and all &c.

'Make Parson Strother stand up for a post!'
Poor fat wretch, his breath will be lost:
Do but consider what sweat it will cost,
If we make Parson Strother stand up for a post,
Black's his coat, and all grey his huge wig,
D'ye think he can move to cotillon or jig?
      No, no, he will pout,
      And he'll dance like a lout,
      And he'll put us all out
      With his carcase so big.
Cho. Susan and Charlotte &c.

'Sweet Lady Bustle, come, you're to call next.'
No, you're out, I'm sure you'll be vexed.
Good Mr Parson, pray stick to your text,
For indeed Lady Bustle is not to call next.
Smart Jack Hobland shall dance an allemand;
So lightly he foots it, by none he's outdone.
      Besides, the 'Bath Gate'
      I have called for, and wait,
      But the man's dunny pate
      Makes him play it all wrong.
Cho. Susan and Charlotte &c.

Oh, could we but foot it to dear Warner's harp,
Tinkle cum tinkle, and sweet flat and sharp;
At our turnings and windings sour critics might curse,
If we could but foot it to dear Warner's harp.
  Oh, my stars! all the couples are out!
  See, pray see, what confusion and rout.
      Mrs Abdy, come here,
      Sister Charlotte turn there,
      Mr Shirley don't stare,
      But mind what you're about.
Cho. Susan and Charlotte &c.

Oh, my dear Charlotte, our dance we give o'er:
The supper-bell rings, and we can call no more;
And Shepherd stands bowing and holding the door,
So you see, my dear Charlotte, we can dance no more.
  See, the servants in grand cavalcade,
  Fruits-compost and sweet crust colonnade.

      See, some carry rusk in,
      And turkey al-buskin,
      And chickens al-gruskin
      In order are laid.
Cho. Susan and Charlotte &c.

Dear Lady Mary, don't kill us with treats,
Patés de veau and transmogrified meats;
Of fish, soup and ven'son the fat Parson eats,
Till indeed, Lady Mary, you'll kill us with treats.
  Mark how clear the choice burgundy flows;
  Brisk champagne sparkles under one's nose.
      The toasts of the day
      Make us all blithe and gay.
      Hark to mirth, hark away,
      Ne'er think of repose.
Cho. Susan and Charlotte &c.

Health, love and joy to the sweet smiling bride:
Bless her, kind heaven, with all bliss beside.
May the hours all laughing serene round her glide,
And give health and joy to the sweet smiling bride.

Guard dear Charlotte too, safe from all harms,
While time moving gently improves all her charms.
      May prudence direct her,
      Till some kind protector,
      Like Hobland or Hector,
      Shall fly to her arms.
Susan and Charlotte and Letty and all
Jump and skip and caper and brawl,
Frisk in the drawing-room, romp in the hall,
Susan and Charlotte and Letty and all.

Margaret Atwood

INTERVIEW WITH A TOURIST

You speed by with your camera and your spear
and stop and ask me for directions

I answer there are none

You ask me why the light here
is always the same colour;
I talk about the diffuse
surfaces, angles of refraction

You want to know why there are
no pleasant views, no distances,
why everything crowds close to the skin

I mention the heavier density
here, the thickness, the obsolescence of vistas

You ask me why the men are starved and silver
and have goggle eyes
and why the women are cold tentacled flowers

I reply with a speech about Nature

You ask me why I can't love you

It is because you have air in your lungs
and I am an average citizen

Fran Landesman

IF THEY CAN'T TAKE A JOKE

I'm not really much of a singer
I try for a high note and croak
The critics may give me the finger
But fuck 'em if they can't take a joke

My act is obscene and offensive
I once made a publisher choke
They can't put me on the defensive
Fuck 'em if they.can't take a joke

True to myself and toujours gay
That's how I am, that's how I'll stay
Sometimes I fly sometimes I fall
But like they say – you can't win 'em all

My love life has been a fiasco
The last was a working–class bloke
I sprinkled his balls with tabasco
But fuck him if he can't take a joke

I've noticed that people are staring
My lyrics disgust decent folk
But my motto is always be daring
And fuck 'em if they can't take a joke

Sappho

'WE SHALL ENJOY IT'

We shall enjoy it

As for him who finds
fault, may silliness
and sorrow take him!

Translated by Mary Barnard

Biographical Notes

Fleur Adcock England
Widely published poet. *Selected Poems* published by Oxford University Press 1983, editor of *The Faber Book of 20th Century Women's Poetry* 1987.

Patience Agbabi Nigeria/England
Poet who has been performing her work for two years. She lives and works in London and believes that poetry should be heard as well as seen. Her poems have been published in *Feminist Review, Black Arts in London, Wasafiri, Class Struggle, Women: A Cultural Review* and *Writing Women*.

Gillian Allnutt England
Author of *Spitting the Pips Out, Lizzie Siddall: Her Journal (1862), Beginning the Avocado,* and of *Berthing: A Poetry Workbook,* and co-editor of *The New British Poetry.* Ex-poetry editor of *City Limits* magazine. Lives, writes and teaches in Newcastle Upon Tyne.

Elizabeth Frances Amherst (later Thomas) (1716–79) England

Adjoah Andoh (1963–) Ghana/England
Born in Bristol, moved to London in 1984. She has been an actor, singer, writer. Lives in Brixton with her daughter Jesse.

Maya Angelou (1928–) USA
Autobiographer, poet, performer, director and teacher. She has written 5 volumes of autobiography, including *I Know Why The Caged Bird Sings,* and 5 volumes of poetry including *And Still I Rise* (1978) and *Sheba Sings The Song* (1987)

Anon
'When . . . one reads of a witch being ducked, of a woman possessed by devils, of a wise woman selling herbs, or even of a very remarkable man who had a mother, then I think we are on the track of a lost novelist, a suppressed poet, of some mute and inglorious Jane Austen, some Emily Brontë who dashed her brains out on the moor . . . crazed with the torture that her gift had put her to. Indeed, I would venture to guess that Anon, who wrote so many poems without signing them, was often a woman.' Virginia Woolf, *A Room of One's Own* (1929).

Margaret Atwood (1939–) Canada
Born Ottawa. Now lives on a farm in S. Ontario. Canada's foremost author, she is a novelist, poet, critic and short-story writer. Her works have been translated into over fifteen languages and include *Survival, The Circle Game, The Animals in that Country, Power Politics, Selected Poems 1966–74,* all poetry, *The Edible Woman, Surfacing, Cat's Eye,* all novels. Also *Wilderness Tips,* short stories, 1991.

Winona Baker (1924–) Canada
Born in Saskatchewan, the sixth child of eight. Moved to mainland DC, fleeing the Depression and still lives there. Over 300 of her poems have appeared in publications in N. America, New Zealand, Japan and the UK. She won an International Literary Award, the Foreign Minister's Prize for Haiku in 1989. Her books include *Clouds Empty Themselves, Not So Scarlet A Woman, Beyond the Lighthouse* and forthcoming, *Moss-Hung Trees: Haiku from the West Coast.*

Maria Banuş (1914–) Romania
Her first collection of poetry appeared in 1937. She is also a translator of Goethe, Rilke, Browning and Pushkin and has published several volumes of essays.

Mary Barber (1690–1757) Ireland
Married a Dublin tailor. Swift admired her verse and agreed to be her patron, which enabled her to publish by subscription *Poems on Several Occasions* (London 1734), dedicated to John, Earl of Orrery. This was well received but brought her little money and in 1738 she again appealed to Swift who allowed her to publish his *Polite Conversations*, which sold well.

Jane Barnes USA
Grew up in Fort Bragg, California, and has lived in Boston for the last twenty years. She is the founder/editor of two presses, Quark Press and Blue Giant Press. She has just completed her second poetry collection *Lamp of the Body*, and is working on a collection of short stories. She teaches writing privately and lives in Cambridge, Massachusetts.

Aphra Behn (1640–89) England
Best known as a playwright, she also wrote poetry and prose. Her first play *The Forc'd Marriage* (1670) was written after a brief marriage and widowhood, a short career as a spy and a spell in a debtor's prison. Known as the first woman to make her living by writing. She dedicated *The Feig'n Curtezan* (1679) to Nell Gwynne and *The History of the Nun* (1688) to Hortense Mancini, a lesbian and mistress of Charles II.

Connie Bensley (1929–) England
Born in South-West London, where she has always lived, apart from wartime evacuation. Has two grown-up sons and works in a Doctor's surgery. Her poetry collections include *Progress Report, Moving In* and *Central Reservations*. She also writes radio plays and short stories.

Sujata Bhatt (1956–) India
Born in Ahmedabad. Studied in the USA and now lives in Germany where she works as a freelance writer and translator of contemporary Gujarati poetry into English.

Jean Binta Breeze (1957–) Jamaica/England
Actress and first woman dub poet, lives and works in Brixton. Does performances and recordings and teaches at Brixton College. She is also a playwright with many playscripts to her credit, and a dancer and choreographer. Her performances are well known throughout Britain; amongst her books are *Answers* (1983), *Riddym Ravings & Other Poems* (1988) and *Spring Cleaning* (1992).

Annie Blue (1951–) England
Born in Preston, Lancashire, now living in London. Writer and painter. Her work appears in *Whatever You Desire*, edited by Mary Jo Bang. She has a daughter.

Debra Bruce (1951–) USA
Grew up in Albany, New York and has degrees from the University of Massachusetts, Brown University and the Iowa Writers' Workshop. Her poetry has been widely published and she is the author of two collections, *Pure Daughter* (1983) and *Sudden Hunger* (1987), which was awarded the Carol Sandburg Literary Arts Award. Currently teaches in the English Department at Northeastern Illinois University.

Nina Cassian (1924–) Romania/USA
Studied drama and painting in Bucharest, she writes books for children and composes music. Has been visiting professor teaching creative writing in New York, and recently in Britain. One of the leading Romanian poets.

Ana Castillo (1953–) USA
Novelist living in Albuquerque, New Mexico. Her work includes *Women Are Not Roses* and *My Father was a Toltec* (poetry) and *The Mixquiahuala Letters* and *Sapagonia* (fiction). *So far from God* (another novel) is to be published by Norton in 1993 and *Massacre of the Dreamers: Reflections on Mexican-Indian Women in the US: 500 Years After the Conquest* is forthcoming from the University of New Mexico Press.

Alison Chisholm England
Has written five collections of poetry, the latest being *Paper Birds*. Her book *The Craft of Writing Poetry* was published in February 1992. She teaches speech and drama and creative writing, and is the poetry tutor for Southport Arts Centre.

Nurunnessa Choudhury (1943–) India
Born in Sylet, Bangladesh. Brought up in a liberal family atmosphere, she soon became involved in the movement for national emancipation. Was the first woman to be arrested and put on trial for her political activities. She has published poetry in Bengali magazines, a selection of poems in *Nakhatrer Protikhai (Anticipating a Star)*, a novel *Gangchill (Seagull)* and a dual-text publication *I See Cleopatra and Other Poems*.

Maggie Christie Scotland
Maggie Christie is from the South of England but has lived in Edinburgh since 1979. Her work has been published by Stramullion, Polygon and Oscars Press. A radical feminist, she helps produce *Edinburgh Women's Liberation Newsletter*, writes and plays music, researches women composers.

Chrystos (1946–) USA
Native American, her tribal affiliation is Menominee. Lives on Bainbridge Island, Washington State. Published in *This Bridge Called My Back*, *A Gathering of Spirit* and various anthologies and periodicals. She has a collection of poems *Not Vanishing* (Press Gang). Involved in political efforts to repeal the Navajo relocation act.

Caroline Claxton (1960–)
Has worked as a Stage Manager. Published in *Girls Next Door* and *Naming the Waves*.

Mary Elizabeth Coleridge (1861–1907)
Born to a traditional Victorian family, her father was a lawyer and a friend of Tennyson and Browning, her mother looked after the household and did charity work. Well-educated in languages, she formed literary groups to discuss writing with others (mainly women). She lived all her life in the family home. Her work was published under a Greek nom-de-plume which translated as 'The Wanderer.'

Gladys Mary Coles England/Wales
Born in Liverpool. Now lives between her Welsh cottage and Liverpool, where she teaches creative writing at the University and in the local community. An award-winning poet, she has published seven collections of poetry, most recently *Leafburners: New and Selected Poems* (1986). Also works as a tutor, critic, editor and literary biographer, most notably of Mary Webb (1990).

Wendy Cope (1945–) England
Born and educated in Erith, Kent. She read history at St Hilda's College, Oxford, then went on to do a year's teacher training. Her first collection *Making Cocoa for Kingsley Amis* was published in 1986 to critical acclaim and in 1987 she won a Cholmondeley Award for poetry. Faber publish her collection for children *Twiddling Your Thumbs* and *Serious Concerns*, her latest collection. Wendy Cope works as a full-time freelance writer and lives in London.

Adelaide Crapsey (1878–1914) USA
Grew up in Rochester, New York. Educated at Vassar College. Spent her life teaching, studying and writing poems. Her poetry *A Study of English Metrics* was published in 1918, after her death in a sanatorium of tuberculosis.

Jo Crayola (1962–) England/USA
Has written poetry since she was very small, and published widely in anthologies and poetry magazines. Works in a sixth-form college, teaching English.

Ann Dancy England
Currently at Sheffield University studying English & Medieval Literature. Wrote and co-directed a play for Yorkshire Women Theatre and the BBC. Published the poetry collection *Painting from Memory*, *Suitcase* and more recently *Opening the Ice*, which is a joint collection with Myra Schneider.

Eleanor Dare (1965–) England
Born in South London. Describes herself as 'a writer, a psychotic lesbian gogo dancer and recidivist trouble-maker'. Works in a public library in London.

Eunice de Souza (1940–) India
Lives in Bombay. Has published three collections; *Fix* (1979), *Women in Dutch Painting* (1988) and *Ways of Belonging: Selected Poems* (1990). The latter was awarded a Poetry Book Society Recommendation in 1990. She is Head of English at St Xavier's College, Bombay.

Emily Dickinson (1830–80) USA
One of the greatest poets in English, she spent her life in Amherst, in her father's house, writing secretly. Of over 1700 poems, only seven were published in her lifetime. She corresponded with Thomas Wentworth Higginson, who twice visited

her. Her chief support was her sister-in-law, Sue Dickinson, to whom she sent many poems. Higginson, essayist, critic and editor tried to influence her to write more conventionally.

C.M. Donald (1950–) England/Canada
Born in Chesterfield, Derbyshire. She went to Cambridge University, came out as a lesbian and feminist in 1976, moved to Canada in 1980 and now works in Toronto as a freelance editor and with the coalition for Lesbian and Gay Rights in Ontario. Her collections *The Fat Woman Measures Up* and *The Breaking Up Poems* were published in 1986 and 1987 respectively; she is co-author of *Talking Gender: A Guide to Non-Sexist Communication* (1991) and contributor to many magazines and anthologies.

Carol Ann Duffy (1955–) Scotland/England
Born in Glasgow. Has lived in Staffordshire, Liverpool and London, where she now works as a freelance writer. Her many awards include first prize in the 1983 National Poetry Competition, Scottish Arts Council Book Awards of Merit for *Standing Female Nude* (her first collection of poems) and the Dylan Thomas Award for 1989. Also published the poetry collections Manhattan (1987) and *The Other Country* (1990) and written two plays.

Grace Evans (1953–) England
Born in the United States to Caribbean parents, she has lived in England since 1969. She is a former member of the Spare Rib Collective and is currently books editor at *Everywoman* magazine. Grace Evans lives and works in London.

U. A. Fanthorpe (1929–) England
Educated at Oxford, has held many writers' residencies. *Collected Poems* published in 1986.

Alison Fell (1944–) Scotland/England
Born in Dumfries. Novelist and children's writer; involved with Women's Theatre; lives in London. Author of *Kisses for Mayakovsky* which won the Alice Hunt Bartlett prize for poetry in 1984, *The Grey Dancer* (1981) (children's novel), *Every Move You Make* (1984), *The Bad Box* (1987) and *Mer de Glace* (1991), all novels; also *The Crystal Owl* (poems).

Janet Fisher (1943–) England
Born in Birmingham, grew up in North Oxfordshire. Moved to Huddersfield in 1978. Now runs The Poetry Business in Huddersfield with Peter Sansom, and has published two pamphlets of poems *Listening to Dancing* (1989) and *Raw* (1990).

Berta Freistadt (1942–) England
Born in London – a war baby. Wrote poetry from an early age and learned how to be good. Describes herself as 'still writing poetry but developing an attitude to goodness that verges on the wicked when she tries hard'.

Anne French (1956–) New Zealand
Born in Wellington, New Zealand, she is currently publisher at Oxford University Press (New Zealand) and is given to satire in her spare time. Her first collection, *All Cretans are Liars* (1987) won the New Zealand Book Award for poetry.

Nilene O. A. Foxworth USA
Poet, author and political activist. One of Black America's most eloquent recitalists. She has written, produced and directed a television show: The Indigenous Woman, and her publications include *Bury Me in Africa* and '*Whose Independence and Whose Liberty*'.

Hayashi Fumiko Japan

Nikki Giovanni USA
Poet, recording artist, lecturer, has been called The Princess of Black Poetry. She has received numerous awards and honorary doctorates from several universities. Her publications of poetry include *Black Feeling, Black Talk* (1968) *Black Judgement* (1969), *Re:Creation* (1970), *Night Comes Softly* (1970), *Spin a Soft Black Song* (children's poetry, 1971), *My House* (1972), *Ego Tripping and Other Poems for Young Readers* (1978) *Vacation Time* (1979), plus others.

Lorna Goodison (1947–) Jamaica
Trained as an artist, she illustrates the covers of her own books. Publications include *I am becoming my mother*, *Tamarind Season*, *Heartease*, *Baby Mother* and *King of Swords*.

Hattie Gossett (1942–) USA
Writer and performer. Lives in Harlem, USA. Her writings have appeared in many periodicals and her poem 'King Kong' was included in Vinnie Burrow's off-Broadway drama *Her Talking Drum*. She has a collection *Presenting: Sister No Blues* (1988). Performs her work with jazz accompaniment and is currently working on a theatre production based on her poetry.

Gwen Harwood (1920–) Australia
Born in Brisbane. Taught music and served as an organist at All Saints Church, Brisbane. She was awarded the Grace Leven Prize in 1975, the Robert Frost Award in 1977 and the Patrick White Award 1978. Published widely, including the collection *The Lion's Bride*.

Jill Hellyer (1925–) Australia
Born in North Sydney. Biographer and novelist. Published *The Exile* (1969) and *Song of the Humpback Whales* (1981). Lives near Sydney.

Cicely Herbert England
Born in Newcastle and now lives in London. She is a founder member of Poems on the Underground and has been a Barrow Poet since the 60s, reading her poems in such diverse settings as pubs, Holloway Prison, an American baseball field, and a Dutch Tram.

Bessie Jackson (Lucille Bogan) USA
A blues and jazz singer of the 1920s and 30s, her songs had strong lyrics which have endured well, although little is known of this artist.

Maria Jastrzębska (1953–) Poland/England
Born in Warsaw, she came to England as a small child and grew up in London. Writes in English, inspired by Polish, her first language. She is the author of *Six and a half*

Poems (1986) and *Postcards from Poland and other correspondences* with Jola Scicinska (1991). Her poems, articles, reviews and translations have been widely published. She is a member of the editorial group which produced *Forum Polek: The Polish Women's Forum*, a bi-lingual anthology of women's work. Currently suffers from ME and says she 'intends to recover'.

Meiling Jin (1956–) Guyana/ China/ England
Born to Chinese parents. Came to England in 1964. Has written several children's stories, and published the poetry collection *Gifts from my Grandmother* (Sheba Feminist Publishers). A black belt in karate, she also enjoys T'ai Chi and has held a wide variety of jobs.

Amryl Johnson Trinidad/ England
Came to England from Trinidad when she was eleven. Her writing, though imbued with a sense of loss, often takes celebration as its theme. Her poetry has appeared in *News for Babylon* and her prose in *Ambit*. She lives in Oxford. She is a graduate of African and Caribbean Studies at the University of Kent. Published *A Long Road to Nowhere* (1985).

Bridget Jones Jamaica/ England
Has been a Senior Lecturer in the Dept of French at the University of the West Indies, currently teaching French at the Roehampton Institute. She has directed plays, and done film criticism for *The Sunday Gleaner*. Her publications include articles on Orlando Patterson and on Leon Damas.

Sylvia Kantaris (1936–) England
Born in Derbyshire. Studied French at Bristol University, taught in Bristol and London and then spent ten years in Australia, teaching at Queensland University. She came back to England and in 1986 was appointed Cornwall's first writer-in-the-community. She has published several collections, her most recent being *Dirty Washing: New and Selected Poems* (1988) and *Lad's Love* (1992). She lives in Helston, Cornwall.

Jackie Kay (1961–) Scotland/ England
Poems have appeared in various anthologies, including *A Dangerous Knowing, Beautiful Barbarians, Dancing the Tightrope* and *Black Women Talk Poetry*. Lives and works in London, teaching and writing and running workshops. Recently published *The Adoption Papers* (poetry), which tells her own story of a Black girl's adoption by white Scottish parents.

Susan Kelly England
Author of several detective novels; *Hope Against Hope, Time of Hope* and *Hope Will Answer*, published in the UK by Piatkus Books and in the USA by Scribner's.

Faye Kicknosway (1936–) USA
Born Detroit. Married, divorced, now lives with her ex-husband and two children. Teaches creative writing.

Ono no Komachi (832–880) Japan
Legendary figure, one of the earliest Heian courtwomen/poets. (Heian-kyow was the old name for Kyoto, the capital of ancient Japan – 1000 years ago a more civilised

and populous city than any in Europe.) The poems were part of a ritual of romance which was a central feature of Japanese court life in the golden age. Ono no Komachi was the outstanding poet, but she died in abject poverty, forgotten, outside the city walls.

Fran Landesman England/USA
Poet. Her collections include *The Ballad of the Sad Young Men and Other Verse* (1975) *Invade My Privacy* (1977), *More Truth than Poetry* (1979) and *Is it Overcrowded in Heaven?* (1981).

Joan Larkin USA
Born in Boston, Massachusetts, and attended Swarthmore College and the University of Arizona. She lives in Brooklyn with her daughter Kate, and teaches English at Brooklyn College.

Julia Lee (1902–58) USA
Blues singer. For some forty years Julia Lee worked as a professional entertainer, mainly in the clubs of Kansas City. She received little recognition during her lifetime – probably due to the risque lyrics she was fond of writing – despite being an accomplished jazz artist.

Liz Lochhead (1947–) Scotland
Born in Motherwell, a prolific dramatist, reviewer and writer. Studied painting at Glasgow School of Art. Her work has appeared on TV, radio and stage. Published several collections, including *Memo for Spring*, *The Grimm Sisters Now and Then*, *True Confessions* and *Dreaming Frankenstein and Collected Poems*.

M. S. Lumsden (1899–1987) Scotland
Born near Inverness. Her poems are published in the collection: *Affirmations: Poems in Scots and English* edited by Evelyn Gavin.

Jennifer Maiden (1949–) Australia
Has published eight volumes of poetry and short stories, her most recent being *The Winter Baby* (poems, 1990). Professional writer, lives in Sydney. She is married and has a young daughter.

OluYomi Majekodunmi Nigeria/England
Born and brought up in Bromley, Kent. Writes, she says, to express and reflect her personal life – racism, sexism and society's pressures.

Chris Mansell (1953–) Australia
Born Sydney. Widely published in literary journals and publications in Australia and overseas. In 1978 she founded *Compass poetry and prose* magazine, which she edited until 1987. Has published several poetry collections; *Delta* (1978), *Head, Heart and Stone* (1982) and *Redshift/Blueshift* (1988). Her manuscript *Shining Like a Jinx* won the Amelia Chapbook Award in the USA and she has another collection forthcoming in Australia, *Day Easy Sunlight Fine*.

Sandra Marshall (1950–) Ireland
Born and still lives in Belfast. Has written several wicked poems which have been
published in various pamphlets and in the anthology of Irish poets, *The Female Line*.
In January 1992 her first full length play 'Molly Moffett meets the Witchbusters' was
produced by the Ballybeen Community Theatre Company.

Bernadette Matthews Ireland
Born in the West of Ireland, her work has appeared in *Salmon* and *Ambit* and she
took part in Eavan Boland's National Writers' Workshop.

Máighréad Medbh (1959–) Ireland
Born in Newcastle West, County Limerick. Has lived in Dublin, where her poetry
was published in the Dublin Writers' Workshop anthologies, *Between the Circus and
the Sewer* and *Edible Houses*. She has also performed her poetry with rock musicians
at various venues in Ireland, including The Underground night club in Dublin. She
currently lives in Belfast. *The Making of a Pagan* is her first collection.

Edna St Vincent Millay (1892–1950) USA
She graduated from Vassar 1917, moved to New York, worked as a playwright with
the Provincetown Players while writing and translating. Her first collection *Renascence*
(1917) was awarded the Pulitzer Prize 1922. One of America's first poets to win a mass
audience for serious writing, her popularity was at its peak in the 1920s.

Alice Moore USA
Black jazz and blues artist of the 1920s/30s. Little is known of her life.

Suniti Namjoshi (1941–) India/England
She has published five books of poetry in India and two books of poetry in Canada.
She now lives and writes in Devon, England. Published widely, including *Feminist
Fables* (1981), *The Conversations of Cow* (1985), *Aditi and the One-Eyed Monkey* (1986).
With Gillian Hanscombe she wrote the sequence of poems *Flesh and Paper* (1986)
available in Britain in both book and cassette form. Her latest books are *Because of
India: Selected Poems* (1989) and *The Mothers of Maya Dip* (1989).

Grace Nichols England/Guyana
Short story writer, journalist, novelist and poet, winner of the Commonwealth Poetry
Prize, and author of two books for children. Her titles include *Fat Black Woman's Poems*
(1984) and *Whole of a Morning Sky* (1986). Her most recent work is *Lazy Thoughts of a
Lazy Woman* (1989). She lives in Brighton with her husband, the poet John Agard,
and her daughter.

Rosemary Norman England
Organiser of the Open Poetry Convecticle, and has been ten years in a women's writing
group. Her first collection of poems, *Threats and Promises*, was published by Iron Press in
September 1991. She lives in London with her teenage son, and works as a librarian.

Dorothy Parker (1893–1967) USA
Poet, reviewer, short-story writer and renowned wit. Her earliest poetry was published
in *Vogue*, for which she then worked. Drama critic of *Vanity Fair* magazine, reviewer
for *The New Yorker* and *Esquire*. Collections include *Not So Deep as a Well* and *Enough*

Rope (both poetry) and *Here Lies* (stories). Twice married, she worked in Hollywood with Alan Campbell, her second husband. After his death she took to drink and died alone in a hotel room in Manhattan.

Lynn Peters (1953–) England
Read English at University College Cardiff and now works as a freelance writer. She has been a regular contributor of poems to Cosmopolitan and writes feature articles for various national publications. She is also involved in comedy writing for television and has contributed to a number of shows.

Fiona Pitt-Kethley (1954–) England
Trained as a painter for 12 years at Chelsea School of Art, and has worked as a theatre usher, film extra and teacher. Her poems have been widely published. Her collection *Sky Ray Lolly* sold out on first printing.

Marsha Prescod Trinidad/ England
Born in Trinidad and came to England in the 50s, where she now lives and works. Her first collection of poetry is entitled *Land of Rope and Tory*.

Vicki Raymond (1949–) Australia/ England
Born in Victoria. Spent her childhood in Adelaide, before moving to London where she continues to live. She won the British Airways Commonwealth Poetry Prize for Best First Volume in 1986 for her collection *Holiday Girls and Other Poems* and has recently been working with the English composer Patrick Morris, who has set to music several of the poems in her collection *Small Arm Practice*.

Sappho (mid-7th century BC) Ancient Greece
Little is known about this most celebrated of poets except that she lived on Lesbos, had a daughter named Cleis, and was highly regarded in her own time, a poet around whom young women gathered to study and perhaps take part in the worship of Aphrodite.

Jan Sellers (1951–) England
Lesbian writer and performer living in London. She works in adult education and teaches creative writing for Goldsmith's College and The Worker's Educational Association. Has performed her poetry with 'Alice's Cabaret' at a range of venues and been widely published in magazines and anthologies, including the title poem for *What Lesbians Do In Books*, The Women's Press, 1991.

Ntozake Shange (1948–) USA
Black poet, playwright, dancer, actress, novelist, director and educator. Books include *Nappy Edges* (1978), *A Daughter's Geography* (1983) and *Ridin' the Moon in Texas* – all poetry; *Betsey Brown* (1985) and the choreopoem which she is perhaps most famous for – *For colored girls who have considered suicide when the rainbow is enuf*.

Izumi Shikibu (974–1034 AD) Japan
Came to the Heian court at the height of its flowering to serve an Empress. Although married and with a daughter, Shikibu began a passionate affair with the Empress's stepson, which proved the inspiration for much of her work. The scandalised reaction to her affair caused her family to disown her. When her lover died she began an

even more controversial affair with her lover's brother. Her poetry reflects her free spirit.

Ruth Silcock (1926–) England
Born in Manchester, Ruth Silcock read English at Cambridge and later became a psychiatric social worker, working with both adults and children. Now lives in Oxfordshire and has published several children's books.

a-dZiko Simba
Founder member of the Munirah Theatre Company, a Black Women's Theatre Company which has performed extensively throughout Britain. Her poem 'Black Coffee and Cigarette Blues' won first prize in the 1985 GLC literature competition.

Stevie Smith (1902–1971) England
Born in Hull. Poet and novelist, her reputation was established through a series of highly successful readings in the 1960s. She published three novels and eight collections of poems in her lifetime. She lived with an aunt in the same house all her life in London, and worked as a publisher's secretary. Won the Queen's medal for poetry in 1969.

Leonora Speyer (1872–1956) USA
Concert violinist, she appeared with the New York Philharmonic and the Boston Symphony Orchestras. She married, lived in London and Paris and had four daughters. She divorced and returned to America in 1915 where she began writing poetry. Her close friend was Amy Lowell. In 1927, her second book of poems *Fiddler's Farewell* won the Pulitzer Prize.

Anna Swir (1909–1984) Poland
Anna Swir was the penname of Anna Świrszczyńska, born in Warsaw, where she was brought up and went to University. Lived in Warsaw throughout the war and occupation and participated in the literary underground. She published nine volumes of poetry and some ten plays as well as works for television and radio. She died of pneumonia after an operation.

Wisława Szymborska (1923–) Poland
Both popular and highly regarded within her native Poland, and abroad, Szymborska has published widely. Her verse, say her translators Krynski and Maguire shows 'delightful inventiveness, a prodigal imagination and enormous technical skill'.

Rachel Annand Taylor (1876–?) England
Rachel Taylor was the author of a pioneering book called *Aspects of the Italian Renaissance*, written in 1923 and recently brought out in a modern edition. Her interest in that period and in art history continued; several years later she wrote *Leonardo the Florentine: A Study in Personality*. She was the subject of a paper given at a literary society by D.H. Lawrence in 1910.

Pam Thompson (1955–) England
Lives in Leicestershire. Lecturer in English at a college of Further Education. Her poetry has been published in several magazines and she was runner-up in the Guardian World Wildlife Fund Poetry Competition in 1989.

Christina Walsh (18th century) England
Little is known of this author.

Helen Watson White (1945–) New Zealand
Born Dunedin, New Zealand. Theatre critic, teacher of drama and New Zealand literature; writer of geography/social history, fiction, poetry and theatre commentary; performer and activist for social change.

Mary Webb (1881–1927) England
Shropshire novelist, poet, essayist and mystic. Her best-known novels are *Precious Bane* (1924), which won the Prix Femina, and *Gone to Earth* (1917). While she won critical acclaim in her life-time, her popular success was posthumous. Her poems have been largely brought to us by the efforts of her biographer, Gladys Mary Coles and are published as *Selected Poems of Mary Webb* edited by Gladys Mary Coles (1987).

Anna Wickham (1884–1947) England
After some time in Australia, she spent most of her life in London. Poems published by Harold Monro's Poetry Bookshop and widely anthologised. *The Writings of Anna Wickham: Free Woman and Poet* appeared from Virago, 1984.

Tzu Yeh (*c.* 4th century) China

Ann Ziety England
Lives in London and performs her poetry and comedy at alternative cabaret venues and Arts Festivals around the country. Teaches creative writing and is education worker for Apples and Snakes Poetry Cabaret.

Acknowledgements

Every effort has been made to trace copyright holders in all copyright material in this book. The editor regrets if there has been an oversight and suggests the publisher be contacted in any such event. The following permissions are gratefully acknowledged:

Fleur Adcock, 'Against Coupling' from *High Tide in The Garden* (Oxford University Press 1971). Reprinted from Fleur Adcock's *Selected Poems* (1985) by permission of Oxford University Press.

Patience Agbabi, 'Rappin' it Up' first appeared in *Women: A Cultural Review* winter 1990, Volume 1 – No.3. Reprinted by permission and copyright © Patience Agbabi, 1990.

Gillian Allnutt, 'Ode' from *Beginning the Avocado* (Virago Press 1987). Reprinted by permission and copyright © for this and 'Thatcherthicky', Gillian Allnutt, 1987, 1988.

Elizabeth Frances Amherst, 'The Welford Wedding' from *Eighteenth Century Women Poets* edited by Roger Lonsdale (Oxford University Press 1989).

Adjoah Andoh, 'c'mon jesse' from *Black Women Talk Poetry* BlackwomanTalk Ltd Box 32, 190 Upper St, London Nl. Copyright © Adjoah Andoh 1981.

Anon, Chinese folk poems, 'I'm eighteen', 'Water Buckets Swing', 'You're like bamboo', 'How can home grown scallions' and 'I sip gruel' all from *Chinese Folk Poetry* translated by Cecilia Liang (Beyond Baroque Foundation 1982). Reprinted by kind permission and copyright © Cecilia Liang 1982.

Anon, 'Poem from Holloway Prison, 1912' from *The World Split Open* edited by Louise Bernikow (The Women's Press 1974).

Anon, 1920 'Down in New Orleans' and 'Diamond Lily' from *The Faber Book of Blue Verse* edited by Philip Larkin (Faber & Faber Ltd).

Anon, 1938, 'She Was Poor But She Was Honest' from *The Oxford Book of Light Verse*, edited by Kingsley Amis and here supplemented by oral tradition (Oxford University Press).

Anon, 12th century AD, 'I like sleeping with . . .' translated from the Sanskrit by Willis Barnstone, and Anon, Morocco, 'An ancient Song of a Woman of Fez' translated by Willis Barnstone, from *A Book of Women Poets from Antiquity to Now* edited by Aliki Barnstone and Willis Barnstone copyright © Schocken Books Inc. 1980.

Maya Angelou, 'Impeccable Conception' from *And Still I Rise* (Virago Press 1986). Reprinted by permission and copyright © Maya Angelou, 1986.

Margaret Atwood, 'Siren Song' and 'Is/Not' from *You Are Happy* Harper & Row, 1974, and 'Interview with a Tourist' from *Procedures for Underground* (1970). Reprinted by permission and copyright © Margaret Atwood, 1970, 1974.

Winona Baker, 'Waiting' from *Not So Scarlet A Woman* (Red Cedar Press 1980). Reprinted by permission and copyright © Winona Baker, 1980.

Maria Banuş, 'The Lost Child' from the anthology of Romanian Women Poets *Silent Voices* (Forest Books 1986, 1989). Reprinted by permission the translators, Andrea Deletant and Brenda Walker, copyright © Maria Banuş.

Mary Barber, 'Advice to the Rev. Mr C' from *Pillars of the House: Verse by Irish Women* (Wolfhound Press, Dublin). Reprinted with Permission.

Jane Barnes, 'Blooming' first published in *Naming the Waves: Contemporary Lesbian Poetry* Edited by Christian McEwan (Virago Press 1988), and 'Routine Checkup' from a new manuscript *Lamp of the Body* by Jane Barnes. Copyright © for both poems Jane Barnes 1988 and 1991 respectively, reprinted by kind permission the poet.

Aphra Behn, 'The Willing Mistress' (1684) from *Poems on Several Occasions With a Voyage to the Island of Love.*

Connie Bensley, 'Faidagery' from *Central Reservations* (Bloodaxe Books 1990). Reprinted by permission and copyright © Connie Bensley 1990.

Sujata Bhatt, 'Shérdi' from *Brunizem* (Carcanet 1988). Reprinted by permission Carcanet, copyright © Sujata Bhatt 1988.

Jean Binta Breeze, 'Dubwise' from *Riddym Ravings And Other Poems* by Jean Binta Breeze (Race Today Publications, ISBN 0 947716 14 9, price £3.50 paperback). Reprinted by permission and copyright © Jean Binta Breeze.

Annie Blue, 'UB40 Queue Blues' from *Whatever You Desire* edited by Mary Jo Bang, (Oscars Press). Reprinted by permission and copyright © the poet. 'If the Cap Fits' copyright © by permission Annie Blue, 1991.

Debra Bruce, 'Hey Baby' first published in *Pure Daughter* (University of Auckland Press 1983). Reprinted by permission and copyright © Debra Bruce 1983.

Nina Cassian, 'Licentiousness' and 'Lady of Miracles' translated by Brenda Walker and Andrea Deletant, from *Life Sentence* edited and with an introduction by William Jay Smith. Reprinted by permission and copyright © Anvil Press and the translators Brenda Walker and Andrea Deletant.

Ana Castillo, 'One Fifteen' translated by Carol Maier from *The Renewal of the Vision: Voices of Latin American Women Poets 1940–1980* edited by Marjorie Agosin and Cola Franzen. (Spectacular Diseases 1987). Reprinted by permission the translator, Carol Maier.

Index of First Lines

I have walked a great while over the snow 50
I help him by taking on the boring jobs, 4
I hear that Andromeda –, 113
I know/you don't want to be eaten, 123
I like sleeping with somebody, 65
I mean, I'm a no shoes hillbilly an' home, 76
I met a Lady Poet, 7
I see a man who is dull, 117
I sip gruel, 143
I swear by every rule in the bicycle, 13
I suspect, 15
I think I enjoyed the party, 119
I thought I'd hid everything, 143
I used to say, 135
I was in a bar once eyeing up the cocktails, 21
'I wandered lonely as a . . . 19
I went into the countryside for a walk, 50
I wish you could be here to see my amaryllis, 71
I write in praise of the solitary act, 36
If, in an autumn field, 66
If you are squeamish, 3
I'm eighteen, 35
I'm equally happy, 131
I'm not really much of a singer, 148
In my church we pray like this, 98
In my dreams, 16
In our town, people live in rows, 65
In red-shuttered houses the down-at-heel whores, 89
Is 'vagina' suitable for use, 12
Is it possible for hours to pass so slowly, 37
It can't have been fun for the Buddha's wife, 94
It is night again, 73
It pays to be a poet, 5
It takes a certain savoir-faire to give a paper on, 117
It was back in the early sixties, 98
It's due entirely to your beauty, 17
Jingle pills, 120
Last night was, 45
Letters fall from my words, 12
Loot, and marked stranger, 79
love said at the dentist's there for her checkup, 140
Love is not a profession, 34
Lovely legs she had, your Mam, 88
Many happy returns and good luck, 140
My black triangle, 67
My friend and I, put out, 92

Index of Poets